CREATIVE LIVES

Edited by

HAROLD E. B. SPEIGHT, M.A., D.D.

~~~~~~~

LIFE OF
PHILLIPS BROOKS

✠

Phillips Brooks

Creative Lives

LIFE OF
PHILLIPS BROOKS

By
William Lawrence 1850-

1930
HARPER & BROTHERS PUBLISHERS
New York and London

LIFE OF
PHILLIPS BROOKS

———————

CONTENTS

~~~~~~

[v]

Contents

Introduction

Phillips Brooks was a leader of youth in the last generation. His was the spirit of adventure in thought, life, and faith. The Youth of to-day are moving up and along other paths and meeting other problems, but the spirit and method of the climber towards light and truth we want to know.

A while ago I was sitting with three vigorous Missionary Bishops from the South and far West: and having this Life in mind I said to each one, "Did you ever hear Phillips Brooks speak? What effect did he have on you?"

The first answered, "Yes, I heard him once talk to a convention of young men, and for the first time realized the nobility of Christ and the glory of a Christian life. I was a young business man then, and here I am."

The second Bishop said, "When I was a choir boy I heard him once. I remember how big he was. There is only one sentence that I recall and that has gone with me through life, 'Flame leaps to flame.'" It describes that Bishop's career.

Introduction

To the third I said, "You were brought up in Trinity Church under Brooks, what do you say?" His answer was, "About all that I am that is good is due to Brooks and my parents, but I wonder if you ever heard this story: A 'tough' was induced to hear him in Faneuil Hall or somewhere, and in answer to the question, 'What did you think of him?' he blurted out 'My God, I believe he would make a good man of me for a week.'"

In the writing of this Short Life of Phillips Brooks I have depended entirely upon my own memories, supported by Dr. A. V. G. Allen's Phillips Brooks, published and copyrighted by E. P. Dutton & Co., Inc., New York, by whose permission excerpts have been taken.

WILLIAM LAWRENCE

*Failure.—Stock: The Phillips Family of An-
dover.—The Brooks Family of Medford.—
Parents and six boys.—Family religion.—Student at Harvard: personal problems.*

ONE day in February, 1856, as Charles
Eliot, then a tutor in Harvard College,
was going up the steps of President Walker's
house he met Phillips Brooks coming out the
door, who brushed by him with a face so pale as
to startle Eliot, who knew him well. Brooks was
then twenty years old, six feet four in height,
loose jointed, awkward but when stirred quick
of action. One's eye immediately sought his
head, which was dominant. It was large, con-
spicuously so because of the lank figure; the
eyes were dark, deep set under a broad brow
which was half covered by an unruly lock of
black and heavy hair; the nose was well formed
and strong; the mouth rather wide and mobile,
quick to respond to emotions of surprise, anger
or mirth; and again ready for a stirring spiritual appeal. The chin and jaw were definitely
strong. Whatever else the young man might be,

you knew that he was virile, honest, sympathetic and likable. It was, however, the tragic in his face that startled Eliot.

Six months before this Phillips Brooks had with the Class of '55 joined in the Commencement exercises, spoken his part and taken his degree, recognized by all as of excellent promise, scholarly, high-minded and with a special talent for vivid and imaginative expression. Hence he was asked to be a teacher at the Boston Latin School, a high honor for one so young. He accepted and in September took up the work. Within four months he failed miserably and completely and was obliged to resign.

His was a public failure, known to his friends, to the schoolboys and their parents. In desperation as to which way to turn he called on the President, Dr. Walker, known for his wisdom rather than for his sympathy. The interview over, Brooks rushed down the steps. His Head Master had once told him that a man who failed as a teacher could never succeed in anything. Phillips Brooks was down and out.

In a delightful address upon Biography given years later to the boys at Phillips Academy, Exeter, Brooks said that "some biographies should begin in the middle of a man's life."

Why not? Why should we want to study a man's ancestry and education before we have met him personally and discovered whether we wish to know him? First a glimpse of the man, then, if he interests us, we study the background, and then the Life.

In this short biography of Phillips Brooks I have followed his suggestion. We have the young man before us. Is it worth while to know him, to go back to his stock and education? In fact Phillips Brooks at the age of twenty was only beginning his real life. He was up to that time little more than the result of his background. With his failure the Phillips Brooks that we know began to be.

Phillips Brooks was in stock, education and character, a typical New Englander. The two names "Phillips" and "Brooks" are saturated with New England traditions.

In 1630 the Rev. George Phillips accompanying Governor Winthrop, Sir Richard Saltonstall, and others, landed from the good ship "Arbella" at Salem. He was a Cambridge University man, received Holy orders in the Church of England, refused to conform and threw in his lot with the Puritans. With others he signed the Farewell Address of affection to the members of the Church of England. Upon the settlement of Watertown by some of the ship's company he became pastor of the church, served fourteen years, and died at the age of fifty-one. Governor Winthrop wrote of him in his journal, "He was a godly man, specially gifted, and very peaceful in his place, much lamented by his own people and others." Then followed Samuel, a Harvard graduate and also a parson, who served the church at Rowley forty-five years. Next came Samuel of Salem, who although a goldsmith held close to the ministry by marrying a parson's daughter, Mary Emerson of Gloucester. From this couple sprang Samuel, a man of "striking individuality and energy of character"; also a Harvard graduate, he was from the age of twenty-two to eighty-four minister of the South Parish, Andover. He married Hannah White, daughter of "the worshipful John White of Haverhill." He turned his hourglass at the beginning of his sermon and ended as the last sands ran through the narrow neck. He was a preacher with power, stood by the ancient Puritan creed and undiluted Calvinism, but "maintained fellowship with the neighboring clergy of a looser and dangerous Creed."

Since 1711 the names Phillips and Andover

have been associated. Samuel's oldest son Samuel, also a Harvard graduate, entered business, acquired some wealth and the official title "Honorable" and built the homestead which has been the home of the Phillips family unto this day. His only son, Judge Phillips, great-grandfather of Phillips Brooks, was a great man: "he had a primary agency in all the measures of the State for nearly thirty years." He had large business in various industries, was for sixteen years a Judge of the Essex Court of Common Pleas; also Lieutenant Governor, overseer of Harvard College for twenty years, received the degree of LL.D. and was one of the original members of the American Academy of Arts and Sciences. He was the projector and really the founder of Phillips Academy, Andover, and into the Academy and Theological Seminary the wealth of members of the Phillips family, male and female, poured. His son John carried down worthily the traditions of his forebears in private and in public life. Dying at the age of forty-four he left thirteen children, ten daughters of whom the sixth was Mary Ann. When a fifth daughter was born to my wife my father wrote her "I suppose that Madam Phillips was disappointed when her sixth daughter was born, but had she known that Mary Ann was to have a son Phillips Brooks she would have been content." Of Mary Ann we shall learn more.

The name Brooks also conjures up New England character but of a different type. The Brooks men were rich farmers, people of trade, as well as of integrity, patriotism and generosity. To be sure, a strain of their blood came from the Rev. John Cotton. Their home was in Medford, convenient to the Town of Boston. Peter Chardon Brooks was perhaps the richest man in New England. He and his people reacted from Calvinism and moved toward Unitarianism.

Peter Chardon was an uncle of Mary Ann Phillips. Hence upon her visits from Andover to Boston she found a welcome at Medford. Her social horizon was enlarged by contact with her cousins the Everetts, Frothinghams and Adamses. Her rare character combined with intense religious conviction won their affection and gave them a fuller understanding of orthodox traditions.

It so happened that a young nephew, William Gray Brooks, came from Portland to enter business in Boston. He too found a welcome in Medford; and there on the Sabbaths and in the evenings of secular days he courted and won Mary Ann.

They were married in 1833 from the homestead in North Andover and set up housekeeping in 56 High Street, Boston. It was a modest house in the vicinity of Fort Hill, which was a center of the larger residences. Their uncle, Peter Chardon Brooks, was near by and the leading churches of the city were in the district. Later they moved into a larger house in the neighborhood; until, driven out by business blocks, they settled in Hancock Street on Beacon Hill behind the State House. Mr. Brooks was a dealer in hardware and earned an income which enabled him to live simply but comfortably, and give the best education to his sons. I remember him well as he sat in the big chair of the "back parlor," a substantial citizen, courteous after the old manner, of deep pleasant voice, well read and of excellent judgment, which was asked in all matters of political and domestic concern. Mrs. Brooks, who though a little bent with age in my time was alert in body and mind, commanded the household by her evident force of character.

The six healthy, restless, active-minded boys demanded of their mother all the love, leader-

[7]

ship and will that the mother had; and she possessed abundance of all; she was supported too by a deep religious fervor which, coming from her ancestry, was by her own prayer and Bible reading kept vital in her soul. To her the church and Sunday services, the Bible Class and Foreign Missions were a chief part of the interest of life. Of course there were daily family prayers read by the father. Among the first memories of Phillips were the stories from the Bible told him by his mother after she had put him in bed. There was no talent for music in the family but hymns were learned by heart and repeated in the circle. Phillips knew two hundred of them when he went to college.

Athletics made up a comparatively small part of boy life in those days and very little was heard of it in the Brooks home. In the winter there were of course skating and coasting on the Common, also "punging" and "cutting behind the boobies" on the streets; and when the boys stayed in Andover the interests of country life absorbed them. "Please tell Georgy that I lost my big large hog knife down in the pasture," wrote Phillips to his mother. At four years of age he went to a small private school; then to the Adams public grammar school and at eleven to the famous Boston Latin School, the first public school founded in this country.

Education was taken seriously. The hours of late afternoons and evenings were given to study, talk upon the lessons and interchange of opinions with their father and mother upon the incidents of the day. When the forty-niners were cradling gold dust in California, Phillips was writing a composition entitled "California," which evidently reflected a popular impression —"the whole country of California for a distance of many hundred miles in all directions seems to be filled with gold."

Great Britain had emancipated her slaves and Phillips at thirteen years of age wrote "Shall North America whose sons fought and bled for their own liberty refuse to do her utmost toward suppressing this infamous traffic which is destroying the liberty of so many of our fellow men?" A sentiment which if expressed upon the Common might have brought him into trouble. His kinsman, Wendell Phillips, lived just around the corner.

In the sixth year of their married life, when Phillips was four years old, Mr. and Mrs. Brooks came to a final decision upon a subject which had disturbed them from the first, their

church connection. It was natural that after their
marriage they should attend the First Parish
Church upon Chauncy Street. It was Unitarian
of a somewhat conservative type. The pastor,
the Rev. Dr. N. L. Frothingham, was a relative of the Brookses; it was the church which
their friends and neighbors attended unless they
had definite reasons for going elsewhere. On
the other hand, the associations of Mrs. Brooks
were with the Orthodox Congregationalists and
her convictions were definite and strong. When
the North Andover parish voted to go over to
the liberal wing her family had severed their
connection and set up an Orthodox parish.
However, in those days the husband was the
official leader even in religious matters. Gradually Mr. Brooks became restless under the
rather colorless teaching of his cousin. Unitarianism itself was becoming more radical and the
unconscious or conscious influence of his wife
was having its effect. Therefore, after listening
one Sunday to a sermon from their pastor of
more than usual radical views, the couple decided that they would not be happy in bringing
up their boys under such teachings. They must
make a change. Where should they go? Orthodox Congregationalism had been driven by the

controversy into narrow and more dogmatic positions. Neither the Old South nor the Park St. Meeting House had the vital spark that Mrs. Brooks looked for. But, as is or used to be the habit of wise couples, they settled the matter by a compromise. In St. Paul's Episcopal Church on Tremont Street they found a service which was somewhat unfamiliar and stately and to Mr. Brooks irksome at first; but the preaching of the Rev. Dr. Stone was evangelical and practical. Hence in pew number 60, enclosed on all sides, between Mrs. Brooks at one end and Mr. Brooks at the door, six boys sat, stood or slouched—kneeling was impossible in those ancient pews. Throughout life Phillips, who at fourteen was within an inch of six feet, had the habit of dropping his head upon his chest and one never knew whether he was asleep or bored or intent with his own thoughts or those of the preacher.

Such a boyhood as that in the Brooks household seems tame nowadays, but it is worth while to glance at the result. All six boys grew to be men of vigor, high purpose and public spirit; taking their part in civic, religious and educational service.

William Gray, the oldest, lived out a long

and useful life as an officer of a Boston bank. Phillips was the second. George, the third, graduated from the Lawrence Scientific School at Harvard; enlisted in the 45th Massachusetts at the opening of the Civil War, and after a service of six months died of typhoid pneumonia. Frederic, Arthur and John all graduated from Harvard, entered the ministry and became rectors and preachers of distinction in Cleveland, New York and Springfield. From their ancestry through their mother these men were filled with an enthusiasm to preach the gospel; in them were emotion, idealism, mysticism and strong character, typical of the settlers of New England. They were a most loyal group; the back parlor of the house where they played, talked and studied, where jokes and laughter were uproarious, was the place to which their later memories turned. Whenever in later years they met they walked arm in arm, leaning on each other; Phillips always in the center if there were three, compelling the passers-by to turn and wonder who they were and what was their joke. To be sure, there was a bit of clannishness in this and their prejudices were sometimes evident though harmless. John was my contemporary and friend. Once in Phillips's later life I said to him, "John says that you are full of prejudices." "Did Johnnie say that?" was his quick characteristic retort. "If you should strip Johnnie of his prejudices you would find nothing but his bones."

In 1851 Phillips entered Harvard. His Sundays he passed at home, as a matter of course. He was fifteen years old and his height made him a marked man and kept him out of what athletic sports there were. He was, however, very likeable, popular in his own circle and respected through the college. Those were the days of Longfellow, Agassiz, Asa Gray, Benjamin Pierce, of whom however he saw little. Younger men, Child, Lane and Cooke in English, Latin and Chemistry were the real teachers. Dr. James Walker, a man of great wisdom and strong influence with the students, was President.

Phillips had no special interest in rank, standing easily about tenth in a class of seventy. He excelled in the classics, reading Greek and Latin for pleasure after leaving college and gaining a reading knowledge of French and German. He read widely outside of his courses and with great speed, having a retentive memory. He was never a real or technical scholar but had a deep interest in studies bearing upon philosophy as applied to life; indeed, life was always his prime interest; hence, he was led to biography. Carlyle was then the master of biography. His *Life of Cromwell* kindled in Brooks an interest throughout life. Milton became to him also another hero. From Tennyson's *In Memoriam* published only two years before, he never ceased to quote. Indeed it sang the heart and yearnings of his generation.

The one feature which stands out clearly in his college work and the testimony of his classmates was his ease and capacity in writing. He was called upon for essays by the Institute of 1770 and the Hasty Pudding Club; he won the first Bowdoin Prize by an essay on "The Teaching of Tacitus regarding Fate and Destiny." In reading these papers one catches occasional glimpses of form, sallies of imagination and a subtle humor which were features of his later style. Frequently too his desire to reduce philosophy, thought and life to simpler forms and spiritual unity appears.

After all, however, he was at graduation much like any other college youth who has sounded the depths while living and talking upon the surface. He was only nineteen, awkward in body

Life of Phillips Brooks

and immature in social and practical life, but in the recesses of his thought problems must have been working themselves out or he never could have developed with such wonderful speed and power in the quick coming years.

What his religious convictions were one can only guess. He was faithful in his attendance at church with his family; listened devotedly to his mother's talk and sympathized with her faith, mysticism and certitude. Doubtless he continued his habit of prayer and Scripture reading. He was most reserved in talk upon religion, took no part in the voluntary religious life of the students and at the same time was clearly a devout and religious man. Conscious as he must have been that his mother was yearning and praying for a public confession of his faith through confirmation and attendance with her and his father at the Lord's Supper, he held back.

The atmosphere of New England was beginning to feel the stir of new movements; Unitarianism had won the cultured of Boston. Emerson and Theodore Parker were in vogue. Brooks never showed signs that he was led their way, but I believe his nature ran so deep, his conscience was so sensitive and his method of

[15]

thought so thorough that he could not take
definite steps which would have to be recalled.
His mother's theology no longer satisfied him,
but her life, her faith and her love of Jesus
did. He had never felt the stirring of a real
conversion as his mother understood it. Commencement was near. Another tradition of the
Phillips family took possession of him, a deep
interest in education. His ancestors had founded
Phillips Academy in Andover. The ambition
to teach the classics and reveal what had come
to him in his study and reading kindled his enthusiasm. He could at least teach. When, therefore, an invitation came to him to be a teacher
at the Boston Latin School he accepted with
keen expectation and with a sense of pride, for
it was high honor to have been selected from
his classmates for that office. The Boston Latin
School had great prestige. His commencement
part given and college life over, he set himself during the summer towards the career of
a teacher; that was to be his life work.

In September upon the opening of the school
he first had charge of a class of small boys, was
then transferred to a group of turbulent lads of
sixteen or seventeen years of age who had driven
out of the chair three teachers. They now eyed

with interest this rather callow, shy and humorous-looking young giant only two or three years older than themselves, who had had no experience in handling boys on the playground or in college life.

The system of discipline under Master Gardiner was most rigid; the ferule lay on the desk ready for use; order was sustained by authority, not by suasion, reason or moral leadership; so it had always been in all schools, especially under "Old Gardiner."

Brooks never had the slightest interest in or capacity for such authority. He went into that schoolroom the unconscious representative of a type of teacher unknown in his day but accepted now: he was, in fact, a generation ahead of his time. The boys could not understand it. When they loafed, failed or disobeyed he reasoned. When they played practical jokes his sense of humor was touched. Disorders increased and he became more and more helpless.

It was a rare thing in those days for a young man to wear eyeglasses. Brooks was obliged to do so when reading; and he had throughout life a unique knack by the invisible shrinking of muscles between the eyes of dropping his glasses off to the end of the cord. What was his surprise one day upon looking up from the morning Bible reading to see cardboard glasses upon all the boys. They threw shot at his glasses. Some years ago a respectable and kindly citizen described to me his method of making spit balls and of shooting them in hopes that they would stick. Brooks would not or could not use the ferule. It was useless to send the boys to Mr. Gardiner for punishment or for him to turn and upbraid them. The cleavage widened and such a breach between teacher and scholars was not unusual in those days. Brooks wrote to a class-mate, "They are the most disagreeable set of creatures without exception that I have ever met with," and later, "I really am ashamed of it but I am tired, cross and almost dead, so good night." By Christmas the situation was desperate and by January hopeless. He was compelled to resign. He had failed. His father wrote sadly in his journal, "The task was too much for Phillips and he is now looking for work."

*Teacher in Boston Latin School.—Theological
Student at Alexandria, Virginia.—Mother and
son.—Rapid growth in original thought: his
graduation address, the charter of his future.*

T H E mortification of Brooks during the
coming months was intense and pathetic.
"Phillips will not see anyone now, but after he
is over the feeling of mortification, he will come
and see you," wrote his father to his rector, Dr.
Vinton. He walked the streets, haunted the
Public Library and Athenæum, took books
home to read, and in the back parlor forgot
himself. He jotted down the names of his classmates and friends, and wrote opposite them
their occupations. His chum, Edward Dalton,
was studying medicine in New York; Charles
Adams was in a law office; Frank Sanborn was
busy in anti-slavery activities; Sawyer was
teaching at Exeter; and he who in college had
reviewed all possible careers, and had chosen
teaching, was a failure. "I don't know what will
become of me," he wrote, "and I don't care
much." "I shall not study a profession." "I wish

I were fifteen years old again. I believe I might make a stunning man: but somehow or other I don't seem in the way to come to much now."

To occupy a part of his time and earn something, he tutored two boys. He had read much and widely in college, and had discovered a talent for literary expression. Now with his future in the mist, he gave himself with intensity to books. As he read, he picked up blank sheets of paper, and upon them wrote his interpretations and sentiments, throwing some of his thoughts into verse. That he was thinking out his future is clear from outcroppings of expressions here and there.

If I am to choose a life for *myself*, which I am to live and for which I am to answer, let the choice be *really mine*, let me say to my advisers: I receive your advice, but no dictation. Without presumption or vanity, humbly, earnestly, and firmly, I claim my own human and divine right to my own life. . . .

I have failed myself most signally in teaching school, but I am not yet quite ready to acknowledge myself wholly unequal to all this wide world's work.

His was a reserved and sensitive nature. Though frank and open in other relations, he unconsciously warned off all questions about himself and his personal religion. "Touch me not," is a phrase which often came to my mind.

No meddler ever meddled with him twice. In this crisis he turned to a few trusted friends. President Walker, Dr. Vinton, and his father advised him to enter the ministry, and he knew that his mother was praying that he would hear the call. He had never consciously or publicly committed his life to Christ: he could not accept the faith in the form or theology of his mother, though to him she was the ideal Christian: he was of another generation. Questions about the Bible, Atonement, and future life were rising. Dr. Vinton's preaching was eloquent, and had great influence upon him, but it was founded on what was to Brooks a fading theology. Frankly, he could not fall into line with the prevailing religious thought of the day. He did not deny: he simply questioned and hesitated to take action. He felt also that the churches were not facing the problem of slavery as Christians should. He was ignorant too of the work of a minister, and such duties as he was familiar with did not interest him. He might preach, but could he preach as he felt and believed, and still remain in the ministry?

Such thoughts and questions shot through his mind, while the ministry itself in its ideal stood before him, beckoning. There were few the-

ological seminaries in those days. Most of the
teachers were elderly ministers. That at Andover founded by his forebears was the strongest. He, however, wanted to get away from
Boston and make a new start. Dr. Vinton had
mentioned the Episcopal Theological Seminary
at Alexandria, Virginia. Its graduates had a
record for piety, missionary zeal and devotion.
Autumn had come: the seminary had already
opened. He must decide to do something. One
day in October he suddenly dropped out of
sight. To a protesting friend he wrote a month
later, "Please let all that matter drop. I said
scarcely anything to anyone but Father and
Mother. Consider me here at the Seminary
without debating how I got here."

On November 7 he arrived by boat from
Washington, for no bridge then spanned the
Potomac, and wrote home:

As the weary traveller paces the well-worn deck of
the good steamer George Washington on its billowy
course from Washington to Alexandria, he sees on
a lofty hill which rises behind the latter beautiful
town a large white brick building. Well, that's just
where I am tonight. . . . My lordly apartment is
a garret in an old building about fifty rods behind
this called the Wilderness. Its furniture at present
consists of a bedstead and a washstand. I looked

in for a moment, threw down my carpet bag, and ran. I suppose I've got to sleep there tonight, but I'm sure I don't know how. . . . I have seen the head, Dr. Sparrow, who is a thin, tall gentleman, with not much to say. So Buchanan is our next President.

The next day he added:

I have slept overnight in my cheerful hole, and am rejoicing this morning in a cold and a cramp. They have the least idea of New England comfort down here of any place I ever saw. I am in the room of a son of Bishop Potter, who seems to be a splendid fellow; at any rate he's mighty handsome. 'Tis an awkward thing this living in a garret.

Thus the future Bishops of New York and Massachusetts settled down to study.

Those who never saw the South both before and just after the Civil War can have no conception of the shiftless and shabby conditions of towns and country, to which a very occasional Colonial mansion gave emphasis by contrast. One word describes it—slackness. And to a New Englander another word follows—homesickness. Brooks wrote home:

The South is a mean and wretched country at best so far as I have seen it. The line seems marked most plainly where the blessing ceases and the curse begins, where men cease to own themselves and begin to own each other. Of course there is nothing of the brutality here, but the institution is degrading the country just as much. All the servants are slaves. Those in the seminary are let out by their Masters for so much a year, paid of course to the master just as you'd pay for a horse hired. . . . Everything seems about half a century behind the age. There is no enterprise or life. . . . It is the most slip-shod place I ever saw.

A young man holding such sentiments and coming from the rationalist shades of Harvard was naturally regarded with some suspicion by the Southern evangelical teachers and students. They had, however, graces which some New Englanders lacked: warm hospitality, good fellowship and gentle courtesy. To these the temperament of Brooks responded. While he joined in the prayer meetings and somewhat pietistic conferences he was seldom moved, although he appreciated the sincerity of spirit and was sometimes reminded of his mother's mystic temper. But there was to him no relief to the barrenness of intellectual life. "Dr. Sparrow was the one man of thought and vision," he once told me; and throughout life he was grateful for his support and sympathy. The others were worthy men of the dry as dust sort. With a few exceptions the students from south and north were below New England college stand-

ards. However, Brooks took up the life with a
buoyant spirit and fell back often upon his keen
sense of humor. He tackled Hebrew, which was
the only classroom work that demanded time.
"Hebrew is a tough old tongue, as independent
as these thirteen states, so that no previous
knowledge of any other language helps one
out."

He was finding the classroom work intoler-
ably easy and wondering what he would do with
his time when the unaccustomed life and food
brought illness. "I tell you it takes down a
man's spirit to be cooped up in this desolate sort
of way." As his letters were read aloud to the
family in the back parlor his mother, Mary
Ann, in the spirit of a Phillips determined that
prayers for her dear boy must be supported by
action. He was studying for the ministry but
he had not yet taken the first essential step
towards it. He had never publicly confessed his
Lord and had never accepted his Master's invitation to His Supper. She must see that that
is done. Hence she made her plans to pass
Christmas in Washington with her boy. Grateful and delighted as Phillips was, he wrote her
at the last minute not to come. The cold was
severe, all the river was frozen, the roads rough.

Nevertheless she came with her son William as escort. Phillips met them and with them passed the night before Christmas at Willard's Hotel.

In the morning the mother with her two boys went to the Christmas service at St. John's Church on Lafayette Square opposite the White House. The sermon over, the administration of the Lord's Supper was begun. The communicants of St. John's, Senators and others, knelt at the chancel rail. Then arose Mary Ann, William and at last Phillips. I can never enter St. John's, that quaint, historic church, without seeing the vision of the mother, holy, determined, loving, leading her gigantic, bashful boy up the aisle and making room for him to kneel beside her. Phillips was now committed to his Lord and the ministry. What she thought of it she wrote him just a year later.

Boston, December 19, 1857

My very dear Child,—

I have stolen away from the parlor, and the girls and boys, and the closing Saturday night cares, into the nursery to write to you; to send you my wishes for a happy Christmas, and the enclosed ten dollars for a Christmas present, and I sincerely wish it was in my power to *double it*. You must take it as a gift of love from your mother, who loves you ten thousand times more than she can ever tell you, or than you can ever know. As Christmas Day returns again I shall think very much of the pleasant one I spent with you last year, and especially of the happiness and gratitude I felt on first taking communion with you. Oh, it was a *happy* day, and my heart was *full* of gratitude that I had lived to see my child confess his Saviour before men. God grant that *as long as life shall last*, he may be his faithful disciple and devoted servant. And although we shall not be with you this year, Philly, I want you to *enjoy* the day, and think of us, and therefore I want you for my sake to go into Washington to church, and, oh, when you take communion, remember your mother. And after church I want you to go to *Willard's* or *somewhere*, and get a *good Christmas dinner*, with some of *my present*, and then when the children are enjoying their *roast turkey*, they can think that Philly *has some too*. Now, Philly, won't you do all this *for me?*—and I shall think of you on that day as doing it, and enjoying a part of my present. We shall think and talk much of you on that day, and miss you, and long to have you with us, and I *know* you will think of us.

. . . . Philly, I *will say* how much you have improved in your character and in your letters the last year. We both notice it, and I believe you will be a blessing and honor to us in our future years. May you be a faithful laborer in Christ's vineyard, and then we shall feel that all the money you have ever had has been *well invested*.

[27]

Many years ago I added to the communion set of St. John's Church a piece of silver, inscribed in memory of the incident and in recognition of the power of a mother's love.

In the following summer when at home Phillips was confirmed. His mother's record is:

Sunday, July 12, 1857.

This has been a most happy day in which I have witnessed the Confirmation of my dear son Phillips, aged twenty-one, at Dorchester.

I will thank God forever that He has answered my lifelong prayers in making him a Christian and His servant in the ministry.

Oh, how happy this makes me! May God continue to bless my dear boy and make him a burning and shining light in His service.

Committed to his future as he had never been before, Brooks now threw himself into his preparation. Everybody was friendly: he had four or five intimates, but in his intellectual life and his reach into the problems of the faith he was practically alone. Hence he was driven in upon himself, and compelled to hew his own path. The result shows that this was fortunate: for there was now revealed in him that prodigious capacity of mental and spiritual absorption which was his through life. His experience in writing notes on loose sheets of paper led him to bring in his trunk a large number of blank notebooks. He set apart the first half of each book for comments and quotations from his reading: the second half was given to the record of his own thoughts, suggestions and conclusions. The fecundity of his mind soon filled the last half, and he turned back to infringe upon the first.

We can see him in his room, no longer in the garret, reading by the light of a tallow candle; then in his beautiful and uncorrected script dashing off page after page of thoughts, illustrations, imagery: poetry too, for he felt that versification could compel finer expression and closer thought than prose. He probably wrote a volume of poetry during his course. Neither prose nor poetry was to be shown or read to others. They were simply the record of his thoughts and interpretations, a means whereby they were cut into his memory, expressions and revelations of himself from month to month and year to year which he could keep beside him, reread and draw from: they were a part of himself. I never knew anyone who had less regard for notes, illustrations and facts for homiletical purposes than did Brooks. Although

[29]

he charitably supposed that such helps to preachers might have their uses, he really despised them, and could not take seriously the men who used them. A sermon was to him a part of the man, incorporated into his very heart, life and experience: it must be his before he could speak it, or his voice would be a tinkling cymbal. Hence these notes: they were more than his arsenal to draw from: they were a part of himself, wrought out through years of experience and testing. It is remarkable, almost startling at times, in reading his sermons, to come upon thoughts, phrases and topics in the exact form in which he wrote them never to be seen by others, twenty and thirty years earlier. The judges and barristers in the Temple at London, business men in Trinity Church, New York, the people of Trinity, Boston, were moved by the thoughts, sometimes expressed in the very words which first moved him in those three years at Alexandria. He spoke them not, of course, from memory, but because they were truths which by enriched experience had become his own, a part of his very self. He was never overwhelmed by the mass of reading that he did or the fresh thought that poured into him. He was always in command. I recall his once saying to me of a popular preacher who was also an intimate friend, "You can always tell from his sermon what is the last book he has read." This could never be said of Brooks.

He had but little interest in a technical preparation for the ministry. It was the preparation of the man, letting technicalities come as they would. Hence his reading and study were wide as well as deep. He sought for truth, beauty and life: and, as the source of them all, for God.

He buried himself in the Greek and Latin classics. Finishing the reading of the *Agamemnon* on a brilliant spring morning, he dashed off the sonnet:

The story's ended: Fling the window wide;
　Let the June sunlight leap across the room.
　How like a spirit it comes through the gloom,
And draws the old black tragic veil aside!
　All day the passion of the Argive queen,
All day Cassandra's fate-words, half unsung,
Like a dark storm-cloud o'er my soul have hung,
　With choral thunders breaking through between.
We've heard the tale a human life can tell;
　Come, hear the stories Nature's heart can speak,
Hear June's rich rhythms die adown the dell,
　And each tree's chorus grander than the Greek!

Cassandra-thoughts, with more than Loxian spell,
Come singing to us from the mountain's peak!

The Church Fathers claimed him. His list of German, French and English classics is a long one. He reached out in various directions for rare and odd volumes. India became so familiar to him that he felt at home there thirty years later. One could fill page after page with quotations, with score on score of book titles.

Our best and strongest thoughts, like men's earliest and rudest homes, are found or hollowed in the old primeval rock. In some cleft of truth we find shelter, and all the strength that has been treasured up in meeting the storms of centuries is made available for our protection.

Truth keeps no secret pensioners; who'er
Eats of her bread must wear her livery too.
Her temple must be built where men can see;
And when the worshipper comes up to it,
It must be in broad noonlight, singing psalms
And bearing offerings, that the world may know
Whose votaries they are and whom they praise.

New thoughts entering the world come as settlers to take possession of a new country. The old primary patriarchal truths are doing their work in the centres of our being, but there is constant discovery of new tracks of territory in human life, where ground is to be broken. Life is developing the energies of thought, while thought is working out the richness that lies hid in life.

Every past deed becomes a master to us; we put ourselves in the power of every act. A deed simply conceived and planned belongs still to the heritage of thought, but when it passes into act there comes a personality to it, we gain ownership in it, and men will give us credit for its good and hold us responsible for its ill.

In the long years when great principles are busily clothing and arming themselves for their work, our short-sighted weakness thinks them idle.

Profusion, but no waste; this is the law that Nature reads us everywhere, and this law must also prevail in all the great economies of life. Some great true principle must inspire our work. There must be no stint of labor where labor will tell for our neighbors' happiness, but no wasteful extravagance of it where it will not profit. Our study must regulate itself by the principle of profusion that is not waste. And so most of all must our *faith*.

Throughout the notes one feels that Brooks's real search was for the truth, and that he has but little interest in truth as simply an end of intellectual or scientific adventure. All ventures theoretical and practical were to him paths leading up to the ideal Truth which he believed is found in God. Hence his familiar illustrations of the sun and its rays, the ocean and the river.

He read and studied not merely as a preparation, but because he loved to learn and absorb; and above all, he was discovering his power and the pleasure of giving out. As at Harvard, he was called upon to write and read papers. His friend Richards says, "His writing had the ease and charm of a master. The words were choice and simple, the phrases were idiomatic, the sentences brief and lucid, the cadences musical, and the thought fresh and ripe, the feeling real." As he closed his reading, Dr. Sparrow was wont to say in a low voice, "Mr. Brooks is very remarkable."

There were times when the intellectual and social barrenness of the life brought on waves of homesickness. He even applied to the Andover Seminary, but received no reply. His mother's letters followed him.

You *don't know how much* we think and talk of you, and desire your well-doing in every respect. Keep *very near* to your *Saviour*, dear Philly, and remember the sacred vows that are upon you, and you will surely prosper. Good-night, my dear Philly, and pleasant dreams. Whether waking or sleeping, never forget

>   Your ever loving Mother.

The Buchanan administration across the Potomac was driving the North to desperation and Brooks, who hated slavery, was living in its midst among Southern defenders. With great satisfaction he put upon the reading room table a copy of the first number of the *Atlantic Monthly*, which promptly disappeared. Discussions waxed hot. His father warned him not to be rash. To listen in the Capitol to the debates was so maddening that he remained on Seminary Hill.

It is clear from his notes that he was realizing his mission more and more keenly. As he wrote he felt the presence of others.

If I knew that I had fathomed all the love or all the wisdom of God, how faith and reverence and trust would fall away from a being that such powers as mine could grasp.

The soul can travel fast. A moment's sunlight builds the bridge for it to leap to heaven, up the shining stairs, and then come back to earth.

We know God's glory only by God's grace, as it is sunlight helps us see the sun.

We must answer for our actions; God will answer for our powers.

[35]

He jotted down texts for future use. Twenty years later I heard them in Trinity pulpit and Appleton Chapel.

Thy people shall be willing in the day of thy power. (Ps. cx. 3.) Willingness the first Christian step.

Have I been so long time with you, and yet hast thou not known me, Philip? (John xiv. 9.)

Ought not Christ to have suffered these things and to enter into his glory? (Luke xxiv. 26.)

They said unto him, Master, where dwellest thou? He said unto them, Come and see. (John i. 38.)

He wrote his brother:

Whether it is this getting at sermon-writing that makes me feel more than ever how weak I am to go about the world's greatest work, I certainly do feel it fearfully tonight. But yet I tell you, Bill, I can't recall many pleasanter hours than those that I have spent in writing my two or three first poor sermons. It seems like getting fairly hold of the plough, and doing something at last. I always have been afraid of making religion professional, and turning it into mere stock in trade when I approached the work, but I have never felt more deeply how pure and holy and glorious a thing our Christianity is, what a manly thing it is to be godly, till I sat down to think how I could best convince other men of its purity and holiness. I do enjoy the work, and with all my unfitness for it, look forward to a happy life in trying to do it.

Gradually, unconsciously, he was maturing one vital principle which he was to help incorporate into the life and thought of his time and whereby he was to lead tens of thousands into a fuller light and more confident faith.

I almost despair of making the middle-aged and young people of today realize the scrappy conception which the younger people of my day, and more so of Brooks's day had of the universe, of life, of the Bible, of society. Organic unity which is to us a commonplace was practically unknown. Our physical body was little thought of as an organic whole. Society was made up of individuals and classes. There was no social organism. Even the stars in their course were allowed a certain freedom of wild movement. Miracles, not the orderly working of nature, were the chief evidences of Divine Providence. The Bible was inspired, every word of it and all on a level of equal value. When William Temple, later Archbishop of Canterbury, wrote in 1862 of the Education of the World, and illustrated it by the rising morality of the peoples of the Old Testament, he was accounted a heretic. In the popular mind the orthodox stood for faith, the Unitarians for works. Brooks, who had been brought up as a boy under the logical system of Calvinism and the rationalistic methods of Unitarians, rebelled at both. Each assumed that there was a finality to their definitions. He had caught from Origen and Coleridge a conception of a faith in God and the Spirit which transcended the limitations of language and leaped into the realm of the imagination, which shot its rays of hope up into invisible realms, which inspired by suggestion rather than demonstrated by logic. It was a conception for which the people of his day were unconsciously yearning; one which was organic and inclusive, not mechanical and exclusive, which assumed a vital relation between faith and life, between nature and what was called the supernatural, between God and man, who is essentially a son of God; which responded to the rising hope of a universe not once created and set going by an Omnipotent God, but which was transfused and transfigured by the spirit of an ever living, ever creating, ever loving God of Truth. Such a conception was unsatisfactory to those who demanded exactitude, finality, and a dogma of the intellect, but grateful to those who looked for a life in the spirit, and who were waiting for the simplification of the scattered, scrappy and individualistic conception of life.

Brooks chose his leaders. After Coleridge came Wordsworth, Maurice, and Robertson, the preacher of Brighton, and Bushnell of Hartford.

The test question of many members of the Church was not whether a statement was true, but whether it was safe. Brooks looked always for the truth and from his early college days he had found in the truth not vagueness or confusion, but simplicity. He believed that Christ, who is the Word of Life, the Revelation of God, came to simplify, to beautify, and to save life.

Hence when he came to prepare his first sermon, he chose for his text "The simplicity that is in Christ." He sent the sermon to his mother and father, who read it and pronounced it "very good and sound" but neither of them caught its implications which were to shake the foundations of the theology on which their faith was built. So sure was Brooks that this sermon expressed his fundamental principles that he read the first half of it as his Commencement part upon his graduation from the seminary.

When we once get within the sphere of a great truth, we find all mental life seeking its center in it—thought and fancy, energy and faith, hope, fear, and speculation, all hurrying to the forum where their business is to be done and their fate decided. It is just as when we come near a great city we see life becoming more and 'more centralized every mile.

And in spiritual no less than in mental life there lives the same deep power. Truth centralizes not Thought only, but Affection and Will. The Soul that lived for a thousand ends sees God's light for a moment, and begins to live for one; the dissipated moral nature grows to a system round its central sun; the aimless study of earth's schools is sanctified thenceforth, for it is a culture of a soul for heaven, and human energy feels the strong finger of God's truth upon it, and stands up in the new dignity of holy zeal.

God's plan has all the wonderful simplicity that makes His natural work so grand. In the center of our life stands the great Christ—truth He has set up, the single fountain out of which all sin and all uncleanness are to drink for healing. Every step that is not toward the fountain is toward the desert.

There is no sinecure in the soul's economy. Every power has its work to do, every capacity its gift to fill, every motive its wheels to turn or shaft to drive in achieving finally the soul's great work; and so the fullest manhood of man's best development is sanctified by God's purpose of man's salvation.

All heaven is working for us if we will, as the little child digs his well in the sea-shore sand and then the great ocean comes up and fills it for him. And here lies all solved before us the problem of Profane and Sacred Study. Looking to this divine simplicity of the scheme of life, to Christ that saves, to God that blesses, no study is profane. Looking away from that central truth of Christ, there is no profaner work than Bible study. So long as the intellect owns allegiance, so long its work is full of piety and purpose, its whole development is a training of the soul that is an heir of glory, against its coronation day.

And with the Intellect the Will and Heart must come. See how the new faith is the resurrection of the life, how the new purpose that concentrates every power in the work of Christ binds the whole human nature closer to the Truth, and closer to its race. Theories and schemes and ceremonies grow tame and dead to the man who has looked the gospel in the face.

This new Christian simplicity is not perfect until it recognizes the world's hope in its own. Then there comes the true "liberality" of our religion. The man begins to identify himself with the race, and wins a share in its collective faith and power. He multiplies his life eight hundred million fold. The world was made and sun and stars ordained, and salvation sent to earth alike for humanity and him. The history of the race becomes his experience, the happiness of the race his glory, the progress of the race his hope.

We talk much of a conservative Church and a progressive Church, of a true and a false philosophy of moral, social, and ecclesiastical life. Let us be sure no Church is soundly conservative, or positively and steadily advancing, that no philosophy is wise and no Christianity Christian where the great centralizing Power, the gravitation that binds every particle of Church and Life to Christ the Center, is robbed of its supremacy.

Linked by the Law of God to that, the Central Fact about which God has systematized His moral world, they find their place and own their mission in working out obediently to it the ultimate perfection of the world, of the Church, and of the single soul.

Phillips Brooks at twenty-three was already a Prophet.

J U N E 30, 1859, was Commencement Day at Alexandria. Brooks read his thesis on "The Centralizing Power of The Gospel" to a large audience which included his father. The next day Brooks and several of his classmates were ordained deacons and on the day following he went to pass Sunday with his friend, the Rev. Alfred M. Randolph, Rector at Fredericksburg, and to preach for him.

Can we conjure up the scene on Sunday?—a typical Virginia city with Colonial houses, shade trees and clouds of dust; the July sun poured down its heat upon the good people wending their way to St. George's Church, whose rector was so beloved throughout the state that he became later, and was for many years, Bishop of Southern Virginia. He was a quaint, scholarly and absent-minded man. The gentlefolk approaching the church greeted their neighbors. The ladies closed their parasols, the men dusted their boots and all entered the quiet and simple church. Behind were the poor whites and in the gallery a few negroes. It was the Old South before the War. The preacher, however, was a young giant from the radical town of Boston, and he a radical too: a hater of the sin of slavery. Only five months later in a town not far distant John Brown was hung, and three and one half years later Fredericksburg was wrecked by the guns of North and South, and her streets and river stained with the blood of the youth of Boston. It was the day before the fourth of July, and a Massachusetts man was speaking to Virginians. We have no record of what he said, but years later Bishop Randolph described the impression made. "In thinking of my impression of Brooks's two first sermons and of the way they were spoken, and also of the impression made upon the many intelligent people who listened to him, I am reminded of these characteristics of his preaching which all who ever heard him will recognize,—a singular absence of self-consciousness, a spontaneity of beautiful thinking, clothed in pure English words, a joy in his own thoughts, and a victorious mastery of the truth he was telling, combined with humility and reverence and love for the congregation. I have heard him often since, and the impression is always the same. He was unspoiled and unspotted by the world, especially by that most dangerous and insidious of all the world forces, the praise of men."

The next Sunday he began his ministry at the Church of the Advent, Philadelphia. Many years later, when advising me about my future, he said, "Do not become an assistant unless you have at the same time a piece of work for whose success you alone are responsible. Learn to carry responsibility early and alone: begin in a city if you can, where you may feel the pressure of the people and the work: begin at a distance from your home, where you may strike out, make your mistakes, and not be hampered by the presence of your early friends." He was evidently speaking from his own experience.

The wardens, alert to get the best young man in the class, had approached him in March, but he gave no definite answer. Dr. Vinton, his former rector in Boston, who had come to the great Parish of Holy Trinity in Philadelphia, was urging him to be his assistant. Finally Brooks declined Dr. Vinton's call, and accepted that of the Church of the Advent, but lacking confidence in his pastoral ability, he set the term for only three months, at the end of which the parish could drop him or continue his services. The Church of the Advent was an average city parish of perhaps four hundred plain people. As soon as Brooks had taken charge he entered upon the duties with the same devotion and enthusiasm that he gave to the greatest works of his life.

Parishes were not then organized as they are now. The two Sunday sermons held a higher relative importance. There were the week-day lectures, the Sunday school, the Women's Missionary Society, the wardens and vestry, and of course the parish visiting.

Brooks is popularly known as a great preacher, and such he was. But in all my relations with him I could never discover that he thought he was. If he ever thought so, he passed his whole life in subtle evasion. He was a great man physically and very normal, and that normality was his at every point. His intimate friend, Dr. Weir Mitchell, said of him, "I have known a number of men we call great poets, statesmen, soldiers, but Phillips was the only

[46]

one I ever knew who seemed to me to be entirely great."

When he began his work he laid out his time like any other parson of these days. Study and sermon work in the mornings, parish calling in the afternoon, while the evenings were given to social life, in or out of the parish, to addresses or reading. Soon people outside the parish discovered the young preacher and the church began to fill up. No comment in his notes or diary other than the entry of "a good congregation" or "a full Church" reveals that he thought of his preaching as attracting them. Indeed, when talking to me years later about his early parish life and of his parish calls he said, "I gained more people and loyalty by one call than in any other way. I found a young mother, tired out and almost ill with the care of her sick baby. I told her to go out, get some fresh air, see her friends and I would look after the baby. She went and, I suppose, told of it afterwards."

Within a few months the church was crowded. Occasionally he preached on a Sunday afternoon in Holy Trinity for Dr. Vinton, and that was crowded. He was ordained to the priesthood in the Church of the Advent on Whit-

sunday, 1860. Invitations to speak for all sorts
of causes and in other churches poured in. Calls
to rectorships came to him from all parts of the
country. It was strange how the word was passed
along, for he shrank from publicity. Then the
rumor spread that Dr. Vinton had resigned to
go to Brooklyn, and that Brooks would be
called. He was called and declined. After a few
months the call again came: he accepted and
took charge on the first of January, 1862.

Here was a young man, only twenty-six years
of age, who had had very little experience in
administration, in the cure of souls, or in preaching, placed in charge of one of the two or three
largest parishes in the Church. Around his personality everything centered. Organizations
were almost unknown. He gave himself to his
two Sunday schools of white and of colored
children with enthusiasm and the utmost care
of detail. He was assiduous in his pastoral calls.
Years later, at a meeting of clergy where
preaching was extolled and pastoral calling
deprecated, I heard him break out with the
words, "I would like to do nothing but make
pastoral calls and meet the people. Indeed if I
did not, I could not preach."

That he did not esteem Sunday morning

preaching his special source of power is seen in the fact that during the first six months of his rectorship of the great, fast growing parish, he wrote only two sermons. He depended on old material, keeping his thought and preaching vital by the many addresses he was called on to give. Then again came months when he wrote two sermons each week, and prepared his Wednesday evening lecture, his Saturday Bible Class lesson, and other addresses. With this said, the fact remains that it was the preaching of Phillips Brooks that won the people, changed lives and gave him his spirtual leadership. When one comes to analyze the sources of such a man's power one is baffled by the subtle and mysterious factor called personality which gives back no definite response. Nevertheless, we can sum up some of the evident sources of the accomplishments of a man so young and untried.

Behind Phillips Brooks were the Phillipses and the Brookses with their spiritual, mystic, ethical and practical characteristics, based on vigorous physique. The prayers and influence of a remarkable mother, the good sense and character of a watchful father, were vital. He had received a strong intellectual grounding in the Boston Latin School and at Harvard. The wide and deep reading of later years, his original comments and poems in his notebooks, his hours of thought and his days and evenings of comradeship all contributed. Enriching and revealing all these was his unique faculty of expression, whereby after once mastering his main thought, Brooks would write and write with beautiful running hand, with imagery and illustration, with historic reference and suggestive phrases page after page which when read from the pulpit lifted his hearers up into realms of idealism, held them spellbound and later drove them to action.

With all this said we have not yet sounded the source of his drawing power as a preacher of the Gospel. He brought to the people of Philadelphia a fresh conception of the Christian faith, one which they were unconsciously yearning for. In later years he brought another fresh conception to the people of Boston and a world-wide circle.

The religious thought of Philadelphia had been along Evangelical lines. Whether the people were Presbyterians or Episcopalians, they were accustomed to the phraseology and theological methods of a tempered Calvinism. These once had vitality and meaning, but now they were worn threadbare and even the most eloquent of the older generation could not revitalize the conceptions of the Atonement, the vicarious sacrifice, eternal life, sin, repentance, heaven, sainthood, the love of God, or the Message of Christ. It was all logical and acceptable to the initiated, but it was not vital, interesting or winning. The little children, the boys and girls who sought the joy of life, and their elders who yearned for a faith enrapt in vitality and action were left out of the system. They slept in the pews. I recall a sermon of his in Boston which he told me afterwards was an old Philadelphia sermon rewritten upon the text "The Beautiful Gate of the Temple" wherein he threw upon the canvas picture after picture of the beauties, joys and graces of childhood. "The Beautiful Gate of the Temple" which opened up into a noble character of manhood and womanhood. Such a thought was as refreshing to those people of Philadelphia as was the cool shower of a summer storm upon their brick sidewalks. It was refreshing to all Christendom of his day. And so, presenting God as the Light of the World, Jesus, the inspirer of all true life at every point, he sent his people back to their homes, offices, schools and play with a conviction of the reality of faith and a buoyance of hope and love. The next Sunday they came again as the traveler to the spring.

At the same time it was all so simple. There were no tricks of oratory, no drawing cards of music or ritual; just the outpouring of the heart and mind of a great personality, fired with the love of God and loyalty to Christ.

We all have a few, a very few vivid recollections of those whom we met once in childhood. I have one. In February, 1862, my father took me to Washington to see the center of the war: those few days were worth more to me than a year's study of history at school. We passed Sunday in Philadelphia, and went to Holy Trinity to hear Phillips Brooks. My father claimed him as one of his Sunday school scholars in St. Paul's, Boston. After the service we waited in the rear of the church. Although I was but eleven years old I can now see as if it were yesterday the young giant leading a few friends down the center aisle, and as he caught sight of my father, his face broke into almost a laugh of recognition; then looking down at me, his eyeglasses dropped as if by magic to the end of the cord, his black eyes shone down, his voice gave welcome, and his huge hand enveloped my small fist. I was a college student before I saw him again, but the man was often before me. My experience was only one of ten thousand young and older people. There was in him a subtle winning personality.

Soon there gathered or swept about him waves of adulation which would have turned any head but his. He did not frown upon it: he lived on as if it did not exist. For years he allowed no photograph of himself to be sold, but pledged the photographers to privacy, giving a few to his nearer friends. As late as 1875, when on a visit from Boston to his old parish in Philadelphia, he called on me, for I was living there then, and in a bashful way drew a photograph out of his pocket with the remark that his friends had compelled him to be taken by Gutekunst, and that perhaps I might like one. One day he tramped up the stairs to Mr. Smith's studio in Boston, so Mr. Smith told me, and sitting down opposite a camera, said, "Mr. Smith, do you ever take a person directly front face?" "We do not like to," was the answer, "but we have to sometimes." "Then take me," Brooks said, "a friend wants it." That is the frontispiece of this book. The photograph of Brooks in a surplice was never public until the photographer died and his outfit was put on the market. He had such reverence for his office that he never allowed himself to be taken in a Bishop's robes: photographs hanging on many walls today are counterfeits, Brooks's head substituted on the plate for that of another Bishop in his robes, I think the innocent Bishop Niles of New Hampshire.

Again and again his mother wrote him, "I had rather hear you praised for holiness than for talent, though of course that is unspeakably precious when used in good service. But, my dear Philly, let no human praise make you proud, but be humble as the Master you serve, and never forget what an honor it is to be the servant of Christ."

"I suppose you feel gratified that you had those two calls, Philly: but don't let it make you proud. Keep humble like Jesus: plead mightily for Christ. Father is very happy in your success, and I wish you could know how glad it makes your mother's heart."

Thus his life in Holy Trinity went on from the first of January, 1862. The congregation increased, and then packed the great church two and three times a Sunday. The Wednesday evening lecture was transferred from the

Chapel to the church, and again it was packed. He preached in other churches near by, and in various parts of the country. He was called again and again to other parishes; was elected to be professor in the Philadelphia Divinity School, and declining, raised among his people the endowment of a chair. Through it all he never lost his sense of proportion, or forgot relative values. He was the minister to the people of Holy Trinity: he carried them in his heart and prayers. He was at the bedside of the sick, and the center of happy social life. He worked hard and long, and put his hardest and most careful work into his sermons.

He was young, unmarried, quick to arouse emotion and respond to it. He seemed to have the world before him: women hung about him. With only one was he intimate, Elizabeth Mitchell, the only sister of Weir, a chronic invalid of rare intellect, wit and character. His one mission was to preach the Gospel to the men, women and children before him in such a way as to make Christ live again in the coming generation. There were hours of depression when his work seemed futile, when his teachings were misunderstood and he was thought to be a radical and a heretic. Even his mother

[55]

had her fears; but with quiet courage and cheer, often with a hearty laugh, he worked on: and "the people heard him gladly."

There was another side to his ministry in Philadelphia that drew from him spiritual forces which without it might never have been freed for service, the Civil War. Brooks hated the sin of slavery with a hot and righteous hatred. He had lived in it at its best, and still he hated it.

Years before he had hailed the raw Westerner, Abraham Lincoln, as a man to follow. He had seen and heard him, and there stands in his notebook in a place all by itself on November 6, 1860, "Abraham Lincoln chosen President of the United States." A year before, he had drawn a heavy line of black about the record, "Friday, December, 1859, 10.15 A.M. John Brown hung at Charlestown, Va." He wrote his brother William, "Well, poor old Brown's gone. What a death for such a man. It makes me mad to hear the way some of our Northern conservatives talk about him. What do people say about him in Boston?" His father wrote saying emphatically that Phillips had better be careful and "not carry his politics into the pulpit." Something which Phillips never did unless moral issues were clearly involved. Philadelphia, while loyal to the Union cause as a whole, had in it a large contingent of Southern sympathizers, "Copperheads," whom Phillips Brooks and every public man who stood for the Union and for Freedom had to reckon with.

He was young, and from radical Boston. He was new in the city, and unfamiliar with its traditions. Many of the Southern sympathizers were of the finest and most respected citizens, some were influential members of his parish. His one dominant passion was that slavery must be stopped; and if the slave power should fight, then, war, a righteous war, was on, for the whole country must be one and be free. He was of the mind of Lincoln.

On April 29 he wrote home, "We see the Massachusetts men as they pass on their way to Baltimore, and in a few hours we hear of their being bruised and beaten and killed in a city that claims all the benefits of being on our side. There can be but one party in the North now. There is but one in Philadelphia."

On September 26 he wrote home, "We have heard the Proclamation of Freedom promised from the President's chair. I am sure for one we may go with the *Tribune* and say, 'God bless Abraham Lincoln.' What do they say about it in Boston?" To which his conservative father replied, "It may be a very good thing, and it *may* prove a mere nullity." All Philadelphia was not of one mind, and Brooks found himself as a citizen involved in the foundation of the Union League Club, in the Sanitary Commission, and in all sorts of meetings and enterprises for the creation of a loyal spirit, the support of the Administration, the care of the wounded, and the defense of the country. Once when the Confederate Army was within one hundred miles of Philadelphia, and the city was threatened, Brooks and a hundred other clergymen stormed the City Hall and demanded of the mayor that they be given shovels and picks to build earthworks. He applied for a chaplaincy, but was not appointed. He was soon recognized as a leader in the city and state.

His first duty was, however, to his own people as their spiritual leader. His weekly sermons were fresh interpretations of the Gospel, calls to a more intelligent and courageous faith, messages of hope, patience and courage; for he was talking to men and women whose dear ones were at the front or had come home wounded, others had not come back. His own brother

George of the 45th Massachusetts died of typhoid fever at Newbern, North Carolina; and the shaft of sorrow struck deep in Brooks and the Boston home. Nevertheless, the routine of Sunday schools, the women's work, and the Bible class all went on as usual. Occasionally, however, as on a Fast Day or a Thanksgiving Day, appointed by the President, he burst forth in burning eloquence against the sin of slavery, in support of freedom, liberty, and the Union. One sermon near the close of the war upon "The Mercies of Reoccupation," the blessings that had and should come to the people from the sacrifice and victories, was of great power. He pleaded for the emancipated negroes, their right to live and to vote. Immediately after the battle of Gettysburg he went to the field and through the hospitals, helping and speaking.

Then came the victories and the supreme tragedy. As Brooks was one of the early followers of Lincoln, so he was by his great sermon after Lincoln's death one of the first to appreciate his whole character and career, and lift him to the exalted place in which the nation and the world now hold him.

"God allowed Abraham Lincoln to stay until he stood at the grave of slavery," he said at a

[59]

great mass meeting at the Union League Club. "God allowed him to stand and look on the land and not see a black face that was not radiant with freedom. Slavery had been blotted out before God called him to his rest. It is for this that we have cause to thank God for Abraham Lincoln."

Impatient at the suggestion that because Lincoln was not a member of the Church he was not a religious man, Brooks launched out upon a thought familiar to him but not to a mass of religious people, that the whole man and not his technical faith was the test of a Christian. "I believe from my heart that if there be a man who has left on record that he was a Christian man, a servant and follower of Jesus Christ, it is he who lies dead in the coffin today." At great meetings, he gathered in his prayers all the experiences, hopes and sorrows of the past four years into glorious pæans of praise, of thanksgiving for victory, and of pleadings for leadership in the nation's future. These special sermons and addresses were published by groups of citizens of his parish and had a wide reading.

Brooks loved the people and caught inspiration from their various emotions. He went to

Washington for the great Review of the Army of the Potomac. At the passing of the body of Lincoln through Philadelphia, he joined the citizens when it lay in state in Independence Hall, and then went to New York and passed the whole day upon the streets following the procession and watching the people.

At his entrance upon the ministry, Phillips Brooks was a great, normal, inexperienced young man, sensitive to human touch, quick to observe, alert to absorb, and with potentialities un-dreamed of by anyone, least of all by himself, as a leader in the city and the state. In five years he emerged from his pastoral, prophetic and civic experiences a really great man, great in his judgment, imagination, eloquence, faith. At that very time his mother's letter strikes a pathetic note. "My thoughts are all dead. Some-times I really feel that nothing but a mother's love remains in me. That will never cease for the dead or the living, and, Philly, now I don't feel equal to writing you. You have got before me now, and this is the course of all Nature. The old stalk is good for nothing after it has yielded its fruit. Just so is it with you and me."

One more war incident remains. Harvard College, which had given of her noblest and richest, planned for a great Commemoration Day, when the whole body of graduates, soldiers and civilians, would join in giving honor and homage to the lives of those who had fallen.

Friday, July 21, 1865, was one of the greatest days in the history of the university, perhaps the greatest. Major generals and other officers, distinguished citizens and alumni made up the assembly. Short addresses were made by Generals Barlow and Devens, and by Governor Andrew. Poems were read by Julia Ward Howe, Ralph Waldo Emerson and Oliver Wendell Holmes. Then came the "Commemoration Ode" by James Russell Lowell, which has become a part of American literature. At the beginning, however, Phillips Brooks, a young man unknown to most, rose and poured forth in praise, prayer and thanksgiving his whole soul in a way that moved the people. As the company left the church, the speeches and poems, even the ode of Lowell did not seem to have touched the hearts as did that short prayer. Thirty years later Colonel Henry Lee, the Chief Marshal of the day, said, "On that day words seemed powerless: they did not vent the overflowing of sympathy and gratitude all felt. But in the exercises came a prayer, a brief prayer of a few minutes, of one inspired to pour forth the thanksgiving of the assembled brethren. From that moment the name of that inspired young man, till then unknown, became a household word."

President Eliot said, "That one spontaneous and intimate expression of Brooks's noble spirit convinced all Harvard men that a young prophet had risen up in Israel." He was the same Eliot who nine years before had been startled by the pallid face of the young defeated teacher who was down and out.

Phillips Brooks was then twenty-nine years of age.

IV

Travel in Europe.—His message in Philadelphia.
—Work for Freedom.—Call to Boston.

IN 1866 a year in Europe was to an American a revelation which no young American
of today can imagine. I know, for I went, a boy,
a year later for a summer.

There were at that time in this country,
roughly speaking, no Art Museums and but a
few works of art in private collections, no handsome houses, no country estates, not even a well-
kept lawn, no large and beautiful churches,
nothing ancient but the hills. The landscape had
no human history behind it and no remains of
habitation except the traditions of the Indians
and a few spearheads. It was 1871 before the
first meeting in behalf of a Museum of Art in
Boston was held, and in his address at that time
Phillips Brooks referred rather pathetically to
what he, a boy at the Boston Latin School, had
gained from the plaster casts of Laocoön and
Apollo. Plaster casts and engravings were all
that we had of a vision of Europe's art. No
methods of printing or illustration brought to

us the colors of the landscapes of Europe except the intense and glaring blue of the Bay of Naples. I well recall the thrill that went through me as I saw the first emerald green of Ireland, the first lawn outside Liverpool, ancient Chester, its timbered houses and the cathedral, then Warwick and Stratford-on-Avon. These scenes now so familiar were then unspoiled by the march of tourists and the so-called improvements of the twentieth century. Modern Paris was in its beginnings: Napoleon III and the Exposition of 1867 mark that era; and as for the Rhine, Rome, Naples, Athens, they were almost as the ancients and the vandals had left them. To be sure, the mountains of Switzerland were the same as ever, but the peasants were peasants, and in their local dress, and no mountain railroads lured a hundred thousand tourists.

Among the many interesting human traits of Phillips Brooks was his anticipation of holidays, even of one day. For a man who was so engrossed, happy and successful in his work, this is rather exceptional. How little his congregation, while held spellbound by his sermon and his final appeal, realized that he had just written home, "Only three Sundays more, and then

I shall be out of the harness." "Have only two sermons more to write, and you will see me." Again and again in his work and reading his thoughts wandered across the Atlantic.

The strain of the war and another year of parish work left him rather stale, and he felt justified in breaking away for a year. He went carrying with him the affection and Godspeed of his people as well as their gift of a heavy purse of gold. From his landing at Queenstown, through the north and then the south of Europe, through Russia and Palestine, he traveled and looked and absorbed, never for a moment slackening his interest and enthusiasm.

Years later, when I was starting for Europe, he urged me to land at Queenstown and go north to see Giant's Causeway. I did so, and long wondered why he gave me such poor advice which cut out three days from the far more interesting County of Wicklow, until after his death I read in his Life that on his first trip he went north to Giant's Causeway: it was the glamour of his first look at Europe which had gone with him and thrown his memory out of perspective. His *Letters of Travel* reflect his enthusiasm, his imagination, and the way in which he brought history and people to life. Interesting and stimulating as was the scenery of nature to him, his first interest was always in man; and these countries, with the ruined evidence of past civilization, brought reality to his studies at Harvard and his reading at Alexandria.

From Dresden he wrote, "Oh, if you could see the picture gallery here. It has the picture of the world which I have waited years to see, Raphael's Madonna di San Sisto." And from Rome, "The greatest statue I have seen is 'The Dying Gladiator.' The Gladiator has a pathos in it of which I had not believed marble was capable." "Few things in old art have given me more delight than the faun faces, that with a merriment and an animal glee which modern life hardly knows, overrun with laughter, as the fountains do with water, everywhere."

His sense of beauty was exceptional, and so was his sense of humor. Just one illustration. As he wrote, Athens stands before us, the Acropolis, the Sacred Road to Eleusis, the Groves of the Academy; and finally, the newly excavated Dionisiac theater: here *Euripides* and *Æschylus* were performed for the first

[67]

time. Line after line sprang to his memory: the actors were before him. He caught sight of "the elegant marble chairs and the names of the assigned occupants sculptured in each. They are the Priests of the City. The clergy had front seats at the Theatre in those days. I sat down in the chair, and imagined the old Reverend who used to occupy it. My brother of Dionysus sat on one side, and his Reverence of Hermes on the other."

Palestine was as yet comparatively unspoiled, and his mother's Bible stories came back to him in manifold interest and solemnity. He writes of Bethlehem, "As we passed, the shepherds were still 'keeping watch over their flocks.'" The scene went with him back to Philadelphia. Two years later (he told me this himself), the organist of Holy Trinity, Lewis H. Redner, urged him to write a carol for the coming Christmas, adding, "if you do, we will call it St. Philip." "You must write the music," was his response, "and we will call it St. Louis." And so it has come that the carol, "O Little Town of Bethlehem," set to the tune of St. Louis, has been sung by millions of children.

For a year he absorbed Europe and Palestine:

and there entered into the texture of his thought and imagination living material which unconsciously reinforced the beauty and vitality of his preaching.

Passing again through England, he covered some of his old tracks, and went to the "Derby." "The Prince of Wales was there, and so was I." He became restless for home and work. The "back parlor" and his mother awaited him. He wrote her, "The great item of home news is one that interests me deeply. Bridget has gone! You only state the bald fact, but give no particulars about her successor. I do not care what her name is, but what can she do? I insist on flapjacks and fishballs."

Brooks came back to Philadelphia like a giant refreshed, and threw himself into the parish life and work. His physical vigor and endurance were matchless: indeed, for the next fifteen or twenty years he was buoyant in spirits, courage, and faith. Speaking as he did with marvelous speed, his written sermons of a half hour were in manuscript equal to those of forty minutes. He wrote one, at least, of these a week; prepared an address or sermon for the afternoon, his Wednesday evening lectures, and other special addresses. And in the evening he preached, probably the sermon of the morning, in some suburban church.

The crowded church and intent listeners made of each service a special occasion, and would have drawn heavily on the vitality of most men. But he thrived under it, and when the service was over, turned to his friends with a greeting as natural and buoyant as if he had just come in from a walk. Indeed, the reaction was sometimes almost boisterous. Earlier and later in life he had times of depression when it seemed as if he were frittering his life away: but not now. Being an unmarried man, he was a frequent guest of his parishioners and others: indeed it was in this way that he entered into their family life. He filled pages of his note-book with fresh thoughts. Public duties and addresses made their demands upon him, and in the years of Reconstruction after the war he found it uphill work to sustain in the people their idealistic attitude towards the negro. His work for the Freedmen drew heavily on his strength. He planned with the architects a tower for the church. His imagination was kindled by a call to be the Dean of the Episcopal Theological School just starting in Cambridge. It is strange how some of the ablest men are blind to their real abilities. There were times when Brooks so idealized the scholar that he felt that he would rather be one than a preacher. This call seemed to open the door; and it was with regret that he closed it and went back to his pulpit.

These were years when his style was more florid, and his sermons more emotional than later: he selected picturesque and suggestive texts, drawing out in an ingenious way the topic of his sermon, which because of that very fact stuck in the people's memories.

The sum of the whole is that during the eight years he was in Philadelphia he poured into the lives of the people and the heart of the city an ever increasing stream of spiritual life and power. What he said and did, what he was, passed on from parent to child, from teacher to pupil, from friend to friend. Religion, instead of being a phase of life, a creed, or a system of theology, was life itself: a power transfusing and transfiguring the whole personality. And this, we must remember, which is so commonplace today was a revelation to the people of the eighteen-sixties.

His brothers were entering the ministry. Fred was taking a large parish in Cleveland. His watchful mother wrote, "Oh, Philly, I am delighted to see my boys so wideawake in such work. There could not anything rejoice my heart more. You seem to be working hard and to enjoy it. Dear Philly, your influence is very wide and good. May your reward be great. I thank you, my dear boy, for all the happiness and honor your high course brings to me. Go on to the end, and only let your last works be even more than your first. There is but one fault in your letter. You do not tell whether you are going to preach the Foreign Mission sermon. Do, and plead strongly the Lord's cause for the heathen."

When I first read this last clause, the memory of Brooks's great annual foreign missionary sermon in Trinity, Boston, swept over me. He made of that sermon a special occasion throughout life. The cause moved him: it was his mother who spoke through him.

Boston and Cambridge had not forgotten the vision of the young man who offered prayer upon Commemoration Day. His mother was, of course, anxious to hear him: hence he occasionally accepted an invitation to preach in St.

Paul's or in Trinity Church, which his father and mother now attended.

Since 1842 Bishop Eastburn had been the rector of Trinity Church, but the parish work and much of the preaching had been done by the assistants, of whom Henry C. Potter, Brooks's chum at Alexandria, was the last. The Bishop had resigned, and Potter had gone to Grace Church, New York.

The wardens and vestry now turned to Brooks and called him; but in spite of urgent pressure from his parents and Boston friends, he felt it his duty to stand by his loyal parish, which was very large and had far more vitality and missionary spirit than did Trinity. A year went by, and again came the call, with urgent letters from his father and mother and many Boston citizens. Much as he loved Philadelphia, and great as was his opportunity there, the thought grew upon him that in Boston where he belonged and whose traditions he knew his life work ought to be, and he accepted. To his senior warden he wrote, resigning, "I have given it thought, carefulness, and prayer, and have tried to decide it in God's fear. I can say no more, and only entreat you to try and think the best of my decision. . . .

May God bless you always, you and all of yours."

He began his rectorship of twenty-two years at Trinity, Boston, on Sunday, October 31, 1869, at the age of thirty-three.

V

*Boston.—Rector of Trinity Parish.—Boston fire
and destruction of Trinity Church.—New Trinity in construction.—Four years in Huntington
Hall.—Growth in power as a preacher.—Westminster Abbey.*

THE change in social atmosphere from
Philadelphia to Boston in 1869 was to
Brooks a very sharp one, like a Boston east
wind at its worst.

In Philadelphia he had been followed,
praised, and adored enough to turn the head of
any other man. He was in most respects the
leading citizen of the city; and though he
shrank from it, a social lion.

In Boston he found few old friends. His
parents were quiet people, and Boston was then
Boston, self-centered, provincial, and delightful to those on the inside. But in his early
months Brooks was on the outside. He was
often homesick, and wondered why he had
moved. His letters to Miss Elizabeth Mitchell,
a Philadelphia invalid, were so filled with
humorous thrusts at the Bostonese that Weir

Mitchell, after showing them to a few friends, decided not even to allow Professor Allen to read them; for Brooks's sense of humor was very keen: his restraint in public and his freedom among friends were a part of his charm. Beneath the surface, however, one could always feel the sincerity, charity, and earnestness of the man.

Holy Trinity in Philadelphia was a great, vital parish, with swarming congregations, large Sunday schools, enthusiastic workers and young people. It was in the center of a resident population: its tower, dominating Rittenhouse Square, had just been completed.

Trinity in Boston was a solemn Gothic structure of granite with a squatty, battlemented tower. It was downtown on Summer Street, a block below Washington Street. Most of the residents had moved away, and business had taken possession. St. Paul's Church on Tremont Street, and Emmanuel Church across the Common on the west, were gathering the people, and there were few children. Trinity was an old parish dating back to 1729: in 1839 its church of wood had given place to this of granite. There was nothing in the warmth of architecture or service to draw people downtown on Sundays; so that a quiet, scattered, and rather elderly congregation occupied the pews on the floor, while the galleries were almost empty.

On the first Sunday in October, 1869, Brooks, as he began his first sermon, faced a large congregation. The people had heard of him, and were inquisitive; and a change was immediate. He was a pastor as well as a preacher, and knew the worth of a solid body of religious, intelligent, loyal people as the heart of a parish. Hence he soon began to give his Wednesday evening lectures as in Philadelphia, and sent there for the pulpit desk from which he had been accustomed to give them.

I was in college at the time, and went frequently. We walked across the ill-lighted Common, down the silent Winter and Summer streets, passed through a narrow alley beside the church, lighted by one flickering gas lantern, entered a square, drab parish hall, and sat on benches. Here, after a short service, Brooks expounded a parable, a miracle, or a paragraph taken from the Old Testament, for exactly thirty minutes. I often timed him; and learned afterwards with what exactness he had laid out his plan, his subject and divisions. I have before

me as I write a number of his notes in beautiful
hand writing, all well ordered, and with evident
movement of thought. Those were the years
when through *Ecce Homo* and Farrar's *Life of
Christ*, as well as Dean Stanley's work, the
Scriptures, the Holy Land, the History of the
Jews, and the incidents and meaning of Christ's
life were gaining a significance and popularity
undreamed of. Christian people of today have
no conception of the stilted and unreal charac-
ters put over on us young people sixty years
ago as Patriarchs, Prophets and Apostles. Brooks
clothed all this material and thought in such
warm and picturesque language that his people
gained a fresh conception of the reality of the
Gospel. Every thought led up to spiritual interpretations of the incidents, and young as well
as old hung upon the familiar stories and facts,
the spiritual truths which he enforced and could
not forget them. The people at those lectures
were the founders of the new and great Trinity.

But what was to be done about the increasing congregations on Sunday? The pew-owners
held their pews, and no strangers had chal-
lenged them. Soon the pressure at the west
doors was felt. Dillon, the old sexton, was a
character who represented the ancient régime:

he had no pleasure in a crowded church, and felt some sympathy with whose who shut their pew doors and let the people stand. "Poor people go up into the gallery," said Dillon: and some went: then the galleries became full. How could he keep the number of strangers down? Brooks tells us, "Dillon's fertile mind discovered a way to reduce the number. He once came to the Vestry room to tell of a method he had devised for the purpose. When a young man and a young woman came together, he separated them; and he expected me to approve the fiendish plan."

It is quite remarkable that although Brooks was preaching three times a Sunday, he wrote only forty new sermons in his first three years. He was feeling his way, as he did years before at Holy Trinity. He preached his old sermons, worked at his Wednesday evening lectures, gave addresses, and put his time into parish work, getting to know the people and their attitudes of mind, and adjusting himself to conditions: he read and studied.

Within a few months it became clear to Brooks and the vestry that the parish church must go where the people were going, or had already gone. With a statesmanlike grasp, the vestry and he selected a site upon the edge of a great desert of gravel, which by the city plans promised to be the center of the new city. Men had been spearing eels through the ice there a short time ago. But the railroad had hauled in from Needham some hills of gravel and dumped it into the water, filling in the Back Bay from Roxbury to the Mill Dam. Streets and squares had been laid out, and clouds of blinding dust swept across the desert to the newly laid out Public Gardens.

There were many difficulties, legal and financial, to be met, and a few real objections of conservatism and sentiment to overcome. Some downtown families were going to be deserted. There was danger of a long drawn-out struggle, when on Saturday night, November 10, 1872, the fire alarm rang out, and the great Boston fire began its work of devastation. Starting within a block of Old Trinity, it swept east and south, across the downtown district to State Street and beyond, partially checked by the granite of the partly built Post Office, and finally stopped by the destruction of buildings with explosions of powder, and by the water at the docks. It backed up to Washington Street, and opened a view of the whole harbor which no man living had seen or dreamed of, and which is now shut out again. Brooks found the faithful Dillon in the church, trying to save what was little worth saving: nothing more could be done; so they sat in the rear, watched the flames lick up the chancel furniture, and then as the heat drew near, Dillon threw open the west doors as if the congregation were dismissed; and rector and sexton went out upon the street. He wrote later "Trinity burned majestically, and her great tower stands now, solid as ever, a most picturesque and stately view. She died in dignity. I did not know how much I liked the gloomy old thing."

On Brooks's way home he was entrusted by a jeweler with two large bags of priceless jewels which he carried across the Common to safety; and in the morning faced his new life work.

An architectural competition had already been held for a new church, and the plan of Henry Hobson Richardson selected. What with the unexplored problem of building such a church upon wooden piles on filled-in land, and of adjusting all sorts of conditions and raising the money, the parish would be homeless for three years, which later extended to four. This interim offered a consummate test of the loyalty

of the people to the parish and its rector, and of
the leadership of Brooks.

With all the losses there were gains. The
losses were evident. The parish had no home:
the Sunday school was in one place, the parish
work in another. Everything was temporary.
Wednesday evening lectures, special Lenten
services, were to be in Emmanuel Church, the
Central Congregational Church, anywhere; for
churches and people were hospitable. Where
could the parish worship on Sundays for three
or four years? Where could the power of the
great preacher reach and hold them?

Huntington Hall of the Institute of Technology, diagonally opposite the site of the new
Trinity was selected. From an æsthetic and ecclesiastical point of view the Hall was forbid-
ding. From the sidewalk the people, aged and
children, walked up fifty steps to the Hall
doors, which opened directly into the faces of
the congregation. The floor, with students'
chairs, inclined upwards towards the rear. The
walls were cold and bare except for a deep frieze
whereon were stenciled drawings of chemists
and physicists at work in their laboratories.
Large windows let in floods of blinding sunlight. The platform was bare except for Brooks's

familiar lectern, which he had rescued from the fire, and a large table for the Lord's Supper. By all standards of art, psychology, and tradition, worship was impossible in such a place. No knee could be bent in prayer. Within four years there would be left in the people no sense of reverence, no mysticism, no sentiment in behalf of worship, or of a church as the beauty of holiness. Meanwhile, across the street these same people were building a church which in a unique way embodied all these things. The anticipation of the church, with the preaching, character, and leadership of Phillips Brooks, held the people, and the parish increased in strength. In very fact the unusual conditions created a sense of friendliness, democracy, and solidarity, which broke down the conservative traditions of Old Trinity. The Hall was open free to all who would climb the stairs.

Brooks himself was more free to express his fast developing thought and theology, and to speak more directly as man to man than from a formal pulpit. He was in the fullness of his physical vigor. "I know nothing of the grace of sickness," he wrote to a friend. He had caught the atmosphere of Boston of that day, had become familiar with the trends of thought, the

prejudices and side currents. He had talked
and heard men and women, boys and girls talk
and had learned much from them. He had
studied and read. His notebook was beside him
in those days, and while his parish organizations lagged for lack of a home, he had time to
gather his thoughts and prepare an arsenal of
material for the sermons of the coming years.

I can see him now, his face young,—he was
thirty-eight, his hair untouched with silver, his
whole great frame alert, his eye piercing into
the center of the congregation, which when
he announced his text, he already had in the
hollow of his hand. I recall sermon after sermon, the text of which a few months or years
before had caught his imagination, and been
jotted down. "There was great joy in that city,"
the city that has heard the Gospel. "Come and
see," the proper appeal to the skeptic to come
and test Christianity. "Some said that it thun-
dered," the profound and the superficial explanation of things.

I was a theological student then with his
younger brother John. We criticized the construction of his last sermon, when he exclaimed
with disgust, "You students are lost sinners,

hopeless to preach to: quick to study the skeleton and not feel the heart."

On the other hand, he realized one day that I was bothered about problems upon the ethics of the Old Testament: the murder of Sisera, Deborah's song, the damnatory psalms. Every young person was raising questions about them. To my surprise, two or three Sundays later, he took up in his sermon the historic development of the Old Testament: the rise from barbarism to a purer and finer faith, and opened the doors of the doubting heart of every man and woman, while the stream of living truth, like light, poured in. Interpretations of the Bible and of Christian faith and creeds were changing fast in those days. We moved along week by week, month by month, dropping opinions, prejudices, and what we had thought were essentials of the Creed; questioning, and then catching a new revelation from a book or preacher. Under these conditions some of Brooks's sermons were to us epoch-making. We could recall the day and the language in which he opened door after door and let in the light. When he began with the text, "Men's hearts failing them for fear," his people were alert: they were the men. When he gave out the words, "One thing

I know," his people who had lost much, but had held on to one or two facts of personal experience, and thereby saved their faith, listened.

As the rush of words, thought and conviction gained increasing force, one could almost hear the walls of tradition, orthodoxy and partisanship fall down. The atmosphere became tense and electrified. The great Scotsman, Principal Tulloch, after hearing him once, wrote home, "I could have got up and shouted."

These were years also when his reputation as a preacher was expanding, and the pressure to preach here and there throughout the country was strong. He refused to scatter his power and become a "star" preacher. He stayed by his people, built up his congregation and parish, and by a third Sunday sermon or others in the week, preached to thousands in the cities and villages about Boston.

His name crossed the Atlantic and on occasional summer visits he preached in parish churches and cathedrals of England. Crowds gathered. His rapid utterance, his simplicity, unconsciousness and reality attracted them. Dean Stanley of Westminster Abbey, one of the most charming and beloved Englishmen of his day, became his close friend. At that time, however, American preachers were rarely asked to preach in the Abbey.

One Saturday evening in June, Mrs. Lawrence and I were sitting in our room in a London hotel when Brooks suddenly burst in. He had married us in Boston only a month before. With a certain bashfulness, he said that he was to preach in the Abbey on Sunday evening, and that the Dean had given him two tickets for seats in the stalls.

A Sunday evening service in the nave of the Abbey is unique. It is at seven o'clock when the sun is well up, and its glow fills the streets and squares. Within the light is subdued, and along the aisles and in recesses is deepening. Upon the choir stalls are candles already lighted to enable the boys to read the music. Through the great west window the dropping sun throws its beams, which, transfigured with color, light up the organ screen, and leaping over that, touch the highest arches above the great altar.

When Brooks preached, the nave was packed closer than ever, every foot of standing room taken. The voices of the choir filtered in from the cloisters, becoming more articulate as they entered and passed up the aisle: then their

[87]

sound was lost in the singing of the congregation and the booming of the organ. The massive figure of Phillips Brooks stood head and shoulders above the men, while the little Dean was completely lost in sight. Brooks found difficulty in working himself into the small medieval pulpit, and placed his manuscript upon a desk made high for the occasion. The Bidding Prayer over, the people settled in their chairs: the voice of Brooks, scarcely heard at first, repeated the text, "Walk in the spirit and ye shall not fulfil the lusts of the flesh."

I had heard him preach that sermon in Trinity, again at Harvard, and accompanying him with John for a Sunday at Yale, I had heard it in Battell Chapel. His topic was "The Positiveness of the Divine Life." So clear, strong, and virile was the construction of his sermons that I could anticipate every point.

The topic announced and the line of thought laid out, he set out upon his work at a terrific pace, and with deep interest and emotion. I have never before or since seen a choir of English men and boys keenly attentive: but the manner of Brooks entranced them, and every eye was upon him, evidently taking in the man if not the sermon. So for ten minutes. The deep shadows became deeper, but no one thought of else than the preacher and his line of thought; when suddenly his voice broke and was lost. He talked on unheard perhaps for two minutes—it seemed an hour: then his voice came back, and although there was a partial shrinking of attention on the part of the people, it was regained again. And so on to the end. As I moved in and out of the crowd, American voices were heard in regret at the loss of voice, and in praise of the preacher: English voices subdued spoke only in broken sentences of the beauty, the wonder and the mystery of it all.

The next morning the Dean showed us over the Abbey, and as was his custom, pointed to his favorite inscription, "Jane Lister, dear child" —amidst the tombs of the mighty. The secret of the Dean's charm and of Brooks's power was in their appreciation of the individual soul, God's child.

Meanwhile, behind a high board fence in an unnamed square in Boston, the walls of Trinity Church were rising, and on February 9, 1877, with Bishop, clergy, and a multitude within and a massed multitude outside, Trinity Church was consecrated.

Its architectural form told its story. It had

unity, strength, deep and broad foundation, large approaches, under its massive tower and in transepts, the congregation was one body, joining in a common worship, and as "faith cometh by hearing," the people were not at distant points in long drawn aisles, but were compact within sound of the preacher's voice. The Lord's Supper instituted by Christ was a Feast, a Feast of the faithful; hence its table was placed in the center of the chancel, and the people knelt all around it. The whole church stood as a symbol of unity: God and man and all God's creation; hence from wall and through window the glorious color of nature blazed forth in glory.

It was a daring enterprise in its day, as original, as expressive and as unique as was the genius of the American people. Drawing from the past, the architect and the preacher, adapting its form to democracy and a living interpretation of the Faith of Christ, the church, despite its many critics, caught the imagination of the country. Here Phillips Brooks was to preach and minister until called to be Bishop, over fourteen years later. When he entered Trinity Church he was forty-two years old.

VI

T H E Boston to which Phillips Brooks came back was in its religious and intellectual atmosphere a different city from the Boston of his boyhood, or even that which he had left fourteen years before.

The echoes of the theological discussions of his youth were still reverberating. The thrust of the Calvinistic system had lost its force, but much of the system remained in the tradition and belief of the orthodox. God, the Almighty, was afar off: the heavens were as brass, and Jehovah was above them. The language of the preachers was much the same as of old, but the vital power had weakened. Every word of the Scriptures was equally inspired, but there was a suspicion that there were exceptions. The two natures of Jesus, the divine and the human, were on two separate planes. Unreality was sapping the faith.

On the other hand, the liberal, the Unitarian conception of the Fatherhood of God was inadequate, and robbed the Faith of much of its mystery and awe; while the thought of Jesus as the inspired man who went about doing good failed to stir the deeper emotions.

Brooks never had a vital interest in these discussions. To him they were expressions of a local frame of mind. He found more satisfaction in an historic church and its ancient creed, but he could not be bound by traditional interpretations; and whether he were called Unitarian or Orthodox was of little moment to him. He was well aware that neither label belonged on him.

In Philadelphia he had not been compelled to enter these discussions, but had developed and preached a Gospel of God's Fatherhood, the Divinity of Christ, and the glory of the Christian life which had brought thousands to a fuller faith and life.

Now, however, as he came back to his own city, walked the streets, listened to the talk, and looked his congregation in the face, he realized that he was in a different atmosphere. The older people were reasonably content in the traditional faith; but the younger, the more vigorous, were confused, and the thoughtful alarmed. Thousands were saying with Tennyson,

> I stretch lame hands of faith, and grope,
> And gather dust and chaff, and call
> To what I feel is Lord of all,
> And faintly trust the larger hope.

Loss of faith in those days was not simply an incident in the development of thought but a disaster, a loss of the soul's life, and of joy. For another element had entered into the reading, thought and talk of everyone. The writings of Darwin, the discoveries of science, were now seeping through the bulwarks of thought and faith. The descent of man from the ape, the ominous word "evolution," struck terror into the hearts of millions. To be sure, the Christian botanist of Harvard, Asa Gray, accepted these discoveries. So did John Fiske, the historian; but he was popularly considered a skeptic. Agassiz did not. Then came the open warfare between science and religion, of which in England Huxley and Bishop Wilberforce were the plumed knights. Which would gain the victory was the popular question, and all intelligent people were called upon to take sides.

During his first year in Boston, Brooks read,

thought and discussed the problems with his friends. Unconsciously he was feeling his way as a preacher; for he well knew that his mission was to lead. The youth of Boston and Cambridge were looking to him. On one point he was clear: that the touchstone of all science and religion was the Truth. For the time it seemed as if science alone recognized this; for the more conspicuous defenders of the faith were dodging questions here and there: questions of the interpretation of Genesis, of the Age of Man, of the inconsistencies of the Scriptures, of the miraculous, of the Love of God, the sacrifice of His son, the reality of a physical resurrection, of heaven and hell; questions many of them still unanswered.

With the frankness, humility, and search for the Truth of the scientists, Brooks was sympathetic; and his soul was harrowed if not amused by the alarms of the faithful. On coming back from England one autumn, he said to me, "I heard dear old Bishop Wordsworth in Westminster Abbey say that cremation by its destruction of the atoms of the body would do away with the truth of the Resurrection; so I have now become a Vice-President of a Cremation Society as a protest against such queer ideas." Yet a large body of the faithful felt, if they did not think, with Bishop Wordsworth.

Brooks faced the situation with perfect confidence that the Faith would not suffer, but gain by every discovery of truth from any source, and that it was for theologians and for preachers like himself to have the courage to adjust the interpretations of the Faith to meet them.

Hence, as he reached one advance post after another, and was sure of his position, he set it forth in the pulpit or his Wednesday evening lectures with all the force at his command. He was not anxious that his system of thought should be consistent from day to day. He was frank with his people, and they trusted him, waiting with confidence for the next advance.

The unique feature was, however, that he seldom argued out the problems. He was not a scientist or exact philosopher: he was a preacher of the Gospel. He destroyed "vain doctrines" not so much by attacking them as by setting forth nobler truths in their place. While others pounded their desks for science, or their pulpits for theology, he, knowing their positions, pushed through with positive, spiritual interpretations, confident that no discoveries, however much they might conceal the Vision of God, could eliminate God Himself. He knew that systematic theology had its value, but for his purposes he had as little interest in it as did his Master. Like Him, he taught by suggestion, and illustration. He described the loving God not by argument, but by the parable of the Prodigal. The theology of Calvin ran in his blood. He faced the questions: Was man a child of Satan or of God? Was man by nature given over to sin, only to become God's child by some process of conversion or the acceptance of some theory of the Atonement? The answer came clearer and clearer as his thought matured that man was by his very birth the child of God. It is suggestive that the only theological volume that he published, the Bohlen Lectures, was entitled, *The Influence of Jesus*. It was not a logical treatise on Christian Dogma, but a seeking for the source of the power of the Christian Faith in the person of Christ. At the opening of the first lecture, he said, "I have been led to think of Christianity and to speak of it not as a system of doctrine, but as a personal force." "The personal force is the nature of Jesus, full of humanity, full of divinity, and powerful with a love for man." "The inspiring idea is the fatherhood of God, and the childhood of every man to Him. Upon the race and upon the individual, Jesus is always bringing into more and more perfect revelation the certain truth that man, and every man, is the child of God. This is the sum of the work of the Incarnation." "Jesus is mysteriously the Word of God made flesh. He is the worker of amazing miracles upon the bodies and the souls of men. He is the convincer of sin. He is the Saviour by suffering. But behind all these, as the purpose for which He is all these, He is the redeemer of man into the Fatherhood of God." "Man is a child of God by nature. He is ignorant and rebellious, the prodigal child of God: but his ignorance and rebellion never break that first relationship." To reassert this fatherhood and childhood, and to reëstablish its power as the central fact of life, to tell men that they were the sons of God, and to make them so actually, was the purpose of the coming of Jesus and the shaping power of his life.

It is not easy for us in these days to appreciate what a fresh and invigorating message this was to men and women steeped in Calvinistic theology. As they sat in their pews, they felt right then and there a fresh hope, and an outpouring of gratitude came back to the preacher as the bringer of good news.

Another conviction sunk more and more deeply into Brooks's thought as the material universe and nature opened up through the telescope and microscope their beauties, wonders and mysteries,—the Presence of God in them and in Man: The Imminence of God. It is no wonder that in his carol, "O Little town of Bethlehem," he called in the stars:

> O morning stars together
> Proclaim the holy birth,
> And praises sing to God the King,
> And peace to men on earth.

His poetic instincts were aroused. While timid theologians were decrying science and trying to adjust its discoveries to their rigid systems, Brooks leaped at the revelations, and there opened for him a new heaven and a new earth, bound together, interwoven by the eternal principles of God's love and righteousness. His possession of these truths was not so much by reason as by the spiritual apprehension of the whole man. He laid hold of them, reveled in them, dreamed them, and lived them. He had worshiped God and prayed to God. Now he discovered that he was living in God and God in him. The whole universe was the living, throbbing expression of his power and love. The whole creation had grown and travailed in pain for the coming of Christ. Man and nature are fellow workers with God.

The whole tenor of his preaching was therefore buoyant. If he went down into the depths and carried his people with him, it was that he might bring his people up again into fuller light.

Indeed, light was a key of his thought. "When the sun rose this morning, it found this great sleeping world here. It did not make the world, it woke it, bade it be itself. It quickened every slow and sluggish faculty. It called to the dull streams and said, 'Be quick': to the dull birds, and made them sing; to the dull men, and made them talk, think, and work."

"This is the parable of light, 'I am the Light of the world.' A thousand subtle, mystic miracles of deep and intricate relationship between Christ and humanity must be enfolded in those words: but through and behind and within all their meanings is this essential richness and peace of humanity and its essential belonging to divinity. Christ is unspeakably great and glorious in Himself, the glory which he had with his Father before the world was, but the glory which He has had since the world was, has all consisted in the utterance and revelation and fulfilment of capacities which were in the very nature of the world on which His life has shone."

Or again, he would ring the changes on the text, "I am come that they might have life, and that they might have it more abundantly."

Another conviction dominant in his thought and preaching concerned the transmission of truth through personality. His *Lectures on Preaching*, which more than any other of his books revealed himself, and which had immense influence here, in England, and elsewhere, bring out the thought. He had, of course, a high estimate of the value of the reason, of the logical outworking of principles in philosophy, science and religion, but in religion the truth was not merely abstract, packed into a system; it became vital only by being passed through and being incorporated in personality; hence the supremacy of the Revelation of God through Christ; hence also the necessity of personal faith and life in the preacher. "Preaching is the communication of truth by man to man. It has two essential elements, truth and personality. Preaching is the bringing of truth through personality. Jesus chose this method of extending the knowledge of Himself through the world. However the Gospel may be capable of statement in dogmatic form, its true statement is not in dogma, but in a personal life, Christianity is Christ." "The truth must really come through the person, not merely over his lips, not merely into his understanding and out through his pen. It must come through his character, his affections and his whole intellectual and moral being. It must come genuinely through him."

It was because Phillips Brooks, great in stature, in mind, in sympathy and in character, was transfigured by the spirit and power of Christ that the people heard him gladly.

True to his definition, Brooks's sermons were a part of the warp and woof of his thought and life. As we have already seen, the preparation of many of them was begun in his seminary life: seeds of thought dropped into his fertile mind, germinated and developed unconsciously, until some day years later an incident, a phrase in some book, a personal experience, brought them into the foreground and compelled fuller expression. Then, it might be one or several

weeks before the preaching of the sermon, he was formulating the thought, and unconsciously gathering material for it.

On Monday mornings a few of his friends usually dropped into his study, where there was talk, sometimes serious, often light, of the experiences of the day before: texts, anecdotes, chaff. Brooks in the center threw in his questions, quick repartees, and laughed at the jokes of Parks, Browne, Franks, and his brother John. Beneath the surface, however, was the insistent thought of his next Sunday morning sermon. He was casting over in his mind which of two or three topics to select, or had already made the selection the week before, and now that last Sunday's sermons were off his mind, he could concentrate on the next. Throughout the week, every hour in the week, waking and sleeping, the topic was consciously or unconsciously coming to germ and fruitage. By Tuesday morning, with notebook and pen, he jotted indiscriminately thought after thought. Wednesday morning he shook them into definite, very definite shape. He built up his sermon with the industry and skill of an artist. The topic was whittled down to its narrowest limits, every word considered for the sermon must have direction and movement, and so from beginning to end gain driving force. His introduction leading up to the topic was so framed as to catch attention and lead directly up to the topic. Thus stated, the framework and divisions were plainly marked out, one, two, three: and the subdivisions, a, b, c: suggestions, thoughts and phrases written under each: and finally a sketch of the conclusion. So thorough and exact was he that he frequently set the number of pages which should be given to each point, in order that there be symmetry and no overrunning the usual time of twenty-five to twenty-seven minutes.

Thursday and Friday mornings he gathered his whole self for the writing. Before his imagination as he sat at the great desk in his beautiful study were his people with eyes intent upon him, his own people and strangers, young and old, listening, living, yearning people. His hand with unerring touch swept over the pages, leaving a script almost as clear as a copper plate. The leading thoughts, the illustrations, were before him in his notes. He simply wrote and wrote. His passion to reach the depths of their souls drove him on and on. The speed of his speech, approaching twice that of a customary preacher, demanded a long stretch of manuscript. Unwillingly he stopped when half or two-thirds through. On Saturday morning, reading over what he had written, and thus getting a flying start, he wrote on and on, never, however, breaking away from his well-built notes. The last line done, he heaved a grateful sigh, gathered his sheets already cut for him in a special way, took from his drawer a spool of thread, and with quiet satisfaction deliberately bound them together in such a way that the pages would turn over without noise or distraction. The manuscript went into the drawer and rested there: mere paper and ink, but instinct with fire, pathos, reason, humor, and passion. The sermon, however, was in Brooks himself, like a banked furnace waiting to break forth with heat.

Throughout the week, and even on Saturday, he gave to those who were with him little evidence that he was anything other than a genial, sincere, friendly pastor: a light-hearted and sympathetic companion. He received his visitors, made his calls, gave other addresses and speeches, prepared at odd hours, read in the late evenings, or whenever he had a chance; and was altogether delightful to old and young. Indeed this ease of manner, so natural to him, was in its way a foil to protect him from the intrusion of the inquisitive, who were ever anxious to know his opinion, methods, and convictions. He was instinctively as wary as a bird. He would shut himself up in close reserve before men and women of charm and worth, but would open his heart and all that was in him to some sincere boy, humble woman, or deep mourner. To his congregation as a whole and occasionally in a letter to a stranger, he would in impersonal language reveal his own personal experiences. As a friend well said, "His congregation was his father confessor." To them he opened his heart and in their unspoken gratitude received comfort and inspiration.

On Saturday afternoon, he wandered about the streets, looked in the shop windows, watched the people passing, dropped in on an intimate friend, talked with the children, and avoided scenes or conversations that would strike down into the real interest of the week and disturb it. The deep current ran below, the light ripples above: and we who met him saw only the ripples.

On Sunday morning he read over his manuscript, and rekindled the embers of his thought and passion, dropped into the Sunday school, and said a few words to the children, and then passed through the cloister into the church.

I should like to conjure up a typical Sunday morning in the first years of Trinity.

Entering the west door, we find the interior more severe than it is today. The chancel seems bare and empty: there are no choir stalls and no baldachino. Red carpet covers the chancel floor and steps. The pulpit, though similar in shape to the present one, is hung with maroon cloth, which conceals a temporary framework of timber.

From that temporary pulpit Phillips Brooks preached to the end of his rectorship. The organ and choir, a double quartette, are in the west gallery. As the organ sounds, the pew-holders enter the Clarendon Street door. The galleries, which by the insistence of the rector are free to all, are packed with people. Promptly at half-past ten all the doors are opened, and the waiting crowd surges up the aisles, entering the pews, and up into the chancel, filling the sedalia around the chancel, sitting upon the cushions of the Communion rail and on the chancel steps, and lining the walls wherever there is room to stand. The people have come in all sincerity and reverence to hear the Gospel of Jesus Christ.

The rector and his assistant enter quietly from the side, and kneel for prayer, as do the people. The organ is silent, then with the rustle of movement, the whole congregation stands, and the rector's voice, "The Lord is in His holy temple," is heard. There is something that touches one's humble spirit, as without processional the service begins and the Confession is repeated. Morning Prayer over, the rector retires to the robing room and exchanging his surplice for the preacher's black gown, enters, kneels at the chancel rail, mounts the pulpit steps during the last of the hymn; he looks wonderingly at the people, feeling their needs and hopes; turns the pages of his manuscript over; then again gazes intently at the people. The hymn over and the people seated, the preacher in a quiet voice gives out the text; then in a stronger voice repeats it, so that all may hear; then he and the people with him "are off." There is no other fitting expression: the torrent of thought, imagination, illustration, conviction and passion is let loose: from that moment to the end preacher and people are united in one intense purpose, to give and to receive the message of the Gospel of that day.

To quote Ambassador Bryce, "There was no

sign of art about his preaching, no touch of self-consciousness. He spoke to his audience as a man might speak to his friend, pouring forth with swift, yet quiet and seldom impassioned earnestness the thoughts and feelings of his singularly pure and lofty spirit. The listeners never thought of style or manner, but only of the substance of the thoughts. They were entranced and carried out of themselves by the strength and sweetness and beauty of the aspects of religious truth and its helpfulness to weak human nature which he presented. There was a wealth of keen observation, fine reflection, and insight both subtle and imaginative, all touched with warmth and tenderness which seemed to transfuse and irradiate the thought itself."

He was Phillips Brooks transfigured through the power of his Master, speaking with sincerity and love for his Master. Step by step he leads the people on: the words and phrases of his sermon have been so burnt into his memory in the writing that he is comparatively free of his manuscript. Then, as he comes to the close and the final tender appeal, his voice, full of emotion, is modulated, while the expectant listeners strain to hear the last word. There is silence,

silence that can be felt. Without ascription and with little other than a whispered word, "Let us pray," preacher and people pray that the message will abide with them. The hymn and benediction follow. Without recessional hymn the people silently move down the aisles, through the doors, and spread throughout the city.

The afternoon service was much the same. The church was packed, but with a larger proportion of strangers. I once asked him how he could preach with the same enthusiasm to the same people Sunday after Sunday. "Oh," was his answer, "I can't do my warden much good: he is a saint already; but it is the unknown stranger in the back of the church waiting for the Gospel that pulls at me." Yet the warden was as dependent upon the message as was the stranger.

Then towards evening, he picked up the manuscript of his morning sermon and took carriage or train to a suburban town or a neighboring city to preach a third time.

For many years, his morning sermon, except on the first Sunday of the month when the Lord's Supper was administered, was from manuscript. In the afternoon he preached a sermon of two or three years back; for he had no artificial qualms about repeating sermons. "A good sermon, like a good poem, may be read again and again," he was wont to say. In later years he gave up his manuscript, and prepared his sermons as he did his Wednesday evening lectures; working out his framework most carefully on one sheet of paper, always of the same size, easily filed, which he folded and put in his breast pocket; though he never looked at it before entering the pulpit, the fact that it was there gave him confidence.

These details from the shop are of value as are the study of the methods of an artist. And the finished product, the sermon of Phillips Brooks, was as unconscious and graceful a unit of spiritual expression as the work of a masterly painter or sculptor.

To a degree the same was true of all his addresses and after-dinner speeches. To the hearers they were apparently extemporaneous and easy. There was, however, always thought and care behind them. The National Chamber of Commerce met and dined in Boston. The speeches were of a high order, some with a light and humorous touch. Brooks seldom undertook to be humorous or funny in his speeches: he seldom told anecdotes: he did not know how, and he was too anxious to get at his real purpose to delay. On this evening—and it was a characteristic speech—he opened with a few words in a light vein, and then swept on, carrying his hearers with him through the history of commerce, its relations to the welfare and happiness of men, its unification of the world, its creation of international understanding. He carried commerce up above figures, and financial policies and prosperity and wealth, and finally lifted his amazed, subdued, and humbled listeners on to the plane where they found themselves as merchants, bankers and statesmen, ambassadors, missionaries, in fact, called by their profession to do their part in ushering into the world justice, honor, peace and good will, ambassadors of the coming Kingdom of God. The guests had never seen it in that way, and the hush after the speech was more moving than the cheers that followed.

VII

The Rectory and friends.—The Club.—
Church Congress.—His stature: his wit and
humor: Helen Keller.—Love of children.—
Death of his father and mother.

A S I was leaving Albany by train one day in the autumn of 1879, I felt a huge bulk behind my seat, and turning around heard the giant voice of Richardson, the architect, exclaiming, "I have found the house for Brooks." "What do you mean?" was my reply. "For months I have been looking for a design of the rectory of Trinity Parish on the lot at the corner of Clarendon and Newbury streets, and this morning I found it: a charming Dutch house in old Albany on a corner. I have a sketch in my pocket. Its front steps, porch and door will be as large and hospitable as Brooks: its fireplace and hearth will be as generous as his heart. Sitting before the fire, he will look across the green of the Technology to Trinity; and he will be where he belongs, in the center of everything."

The rectory when built was only two and a

half stories high, and was all that Richardson
had said. To be sure, it had no reception room
for callers, only an alcove off the hall. There
was no room or even desk space for a secretary,
but Brooks did not like secretaries: until he was
Bishop he wrote all letters with his own hand,
and was noted for his promptness of response.
In the parish rooms at the church was the parish
staff: like a good administrator he counseled
with them, trusted them, and then went back
to the Rectory which was the spiritual center
of the Parish, and to some extent of New
England: for here friends, parishioners, and
seekers for advice, help, jobs, or the truth, or
inspiration and comfort, found him. He was
open at any and all hours to them all. How he
ever wrote his sermons was a constant wonder
to his friends. He had, however, great capacity
for switching his mind from one track to another: and in those now forgotten days people
had some respect for a pastor's morning hours.

The study was the feature of the house: its
windows giving out upon the streets to south
and west: its coloring warm and hospitable. Over
the broad window was a rich frieze of dead
gold and sunflowers painted by his friend, Mrs.
Whitman, to whom he wrote after long wait-

ing, "Art is long and time is fleeting." Books
were everywhere, in cases, on tables: portraits
of his heroes, etchings, engravings, and photographs of his friends and children covered the
walls and stood on the mantel and tables. A
bronze replica of Lincoln's great fist, death
masks of Lincoln and Cromwell; marble busts
of Coleridge and Kingsley; a graceful image
of Pico of Mirandola carved in wood, bronzes
from India, bric-a-brac beautiful and grotesque:
a little child's doll: every sort of thing was
there, but nothing that did not have the charm
and touch of his intimate knowledge and taste.
It was his, and as he stood before the fire and
talked to the one or ten friends who might be
there, he was evidently the master of the house.
The desk of his friend Dean Stanley sent him
from Westminster stood near by, and his own
great desk whereon he wrote his sermons was
nearer the door. For as soon as a friend ap-
peared he wished to be quick to give him welcome. How vividly I recall the way in which
he looked up from his manuscript, dropped his
pen, let fall his eyeglasses on their string, put
out his huge hand and looked towards a com-
fortable chair: grasping the poker, he broke the
cannel coal into a blaze, and then the talk began

as if there were nothing to be done. And the friend or the stranger believed that Brooks was interested only in him, his talk or problems.

In his study the Clericus Club met once a month: "*The* Club" he always called it: to him it was the only club. Fifteen to thirty congenial clergymen met; one read a paper; then followed discussion which he always closed, then supper. He read papers now published, such as that entitled "Heresy," wherein from the Scriptures and history he showed that its real significance is not intellectual error but a moral fault. "It is the self will of the intellect, the will to believe what we want to, and not seek first what is true." "The Pulpit and Popular Skepticism," wherein he revealed his own method in meeting modern doubt. His essay on "Tolerance" he afterwards expanded in two remarkable lectures given before the University of Cambridge; he pressed home the thesis that tolerance, not toleration, included two essential elements: positive conviction and sympathy with those whose convictions differ from our own. At the Clericus, Professor A. V. G. Allen read the first chapter of *The Continuity of Christian Thought*, and William Huntington tested out for the first time his suggestions for the *Revision of the Prayer Book.*

Brooks was a firm believer in the worth of discussion in the search for the Truth. Fifty and sixty years ago the sentiment and habits of thought and belief in the Episcopal Church were firmly molded, rigid: any question of the accepted opinions was frowned upon, and a protest silenced; with the usual result, much suppressed heresy. A sharp difference on certain interpretations resulted in the creation of "The Reformed Episcopal Church." To meet this risk from suppression, Brooks joined with other adventurous spirits in the forming of "The Church Congress," an informal organization for the discussion of problems of theology and church life and administration. The lid once lifted much heat was allowed to escape and the Congress has been a large factor in giving a feeling of breadth and roominess, which without the loss of its deeper convictions is recognized today as a characteristic of the Episcopal Church. In whatever part of the country the Church Congress held its annual meetings, Brooks was always there, and of course could be trusted to defend freedom of speech.

He was an ardent believer in the unity of the

church defined as "A Congregation of faithful
men," but he had little interest in the unification of different churches by amalgamation or
federation. His emphasis was upon Unity of
the Spirit. He was strictly loyal to what he believed to be the principles and laws of his own
church. In spite of protest from the conservative
leaders of that day, he claimed the right to
preach anywhere; his sermon in the Old South
Church every Good Friday evening was an institution. And yet, though recognized by ministers of all denominations as sympathetic and
full of the Spirit of Unity, he never asked the
minister of another church to preach in Trinity
Church, for he did not think that the laws of
his church at that time allowed it, and he had
no great confidence in exchange of pulpits as a
factor in Christian Unity.

When Phillips Brooks walked the streets of
any city, people turned and looked at him. He
was physically a great man: in build, kindliness
of manner and dignity, he suggested a gigantic
mold. He was conscious of it and took the con-
sequences with good nature, often with real
humor. I speak only of instances caught from
my own observation or told me by himself.
Standing with him at a railroad station, I saw

approaching a big hulky man who in a natural way said, "Stranger, how much do you weigh?" Just as naturally came the answer; and both walked off satisfied. Sitting at breakfast in Paris, he heard the genial voice of William McVickar, "Brooks, I have just been weighed." "How much?" "Three hundred," and Brooks dropped his knife and fork, went to the scales and coming back said, "Just three hundred pounds too." Their fellow traveler, Richardson, weighed more. At the Lido, the three conspirators planned a surprise. First McVickar approached the keeper of the bathing machines and asked for a bathing suit. The Italian was nonplussed. He had never seen such a man, he had no suit to fit him and McVickar walked off indignant. In a short time Brooks approached the keeper with the same request, added that he was an American, that Americans had a right to bathe, and with the same result: the Italian, chagrined and excited, protested, and Brooks retired. Then came Richardson with his huge bulk and stentorian voice. The Italian became wild, a crowd collected, and in high dudgeon Richardson walked off while the people wondered at the gigantic stature of Americans. At Amsterdam, Brooks stood in the Square, admiring the façade of the Stadhuis: a few people gathered about him, the group enlarged, and after some animated discussion, a man ran down a side street. Brooks waited to see the result and soon the man came back accompanied by a Dutchman worthy of Tenier's largest brush and stood him beside Brooks. In subdued voices the Dutch accepted their defeat.

When Brooks was traveling in Sweden, as the boat approached Christiania, he noticed upon the dock a crowd with one handsome man standing head and shoulders above it, Prince Oscar. As he boarded the boat between lines of soldiers and sailors, he accosted Brooks pleasantly, "It is a loyal people, is it not?" In the evening while Brooks was sitting on deck, the Prince left his private deck and greeted him again, talking well into the night. In the morning as he landed, he waved his hand to Brooks, "Au revoir, the world is round and we shall meet again."

Of kindly wit and quick repartee he was a master. Holding this in abeyance in public, he gave himself free play among his friends. Unreality in any form brought forth from him either anger or humor, usually the latter. Shafts of kindly ridicule would dart after commonplace men and women who, impressed with their own importance or talents, adopted an important or solemn manner. He was sometimes too quick in his judgment and prejudiced: but of ill will or malice he had none. Some self-conscious Bishops were his delight, and even men for whom he had high respect and affection served his humor well. Of a new book by a professor whose manner and style he disliked, he exclaimed, "Snipe on toast." He was fond of repeating the welcome of a very old teacher, "How are you, Mr. Brooks, and your family, are any of your friends well?" I met him in Harvard Square one morning after a dinner party at James Russell Lowell's. "Dull dinner," he said. I protested that one distinguished professor had tried his best to brighten it. "Yes," he answered, "he told us that art is gone, patriotism is gone, religion is gone. What are you going to do with a man like that?" As we were driving together over Harvard Bridge to Mr. Lowell's funeral, he caught sight of a new stone church on the edge of the river embankment. "What church is that?" he asked. "The Mount Vernon Congregational Church," I said. "It ought to be a Baptist; convenient to the river."

Dependent as he was upon intimate companionships, he was a silent man in a large company; when he was bored by foolish talk and vulgar people, the atmosphere became chilled, and neither he nor they enjoyed themselves. But in a congenial group, his talk, laugh, repartee, and sympathetic words were fresh and exhilarating; he kindled others to better talk. Nevertheless in much of his thought, ideals and faith he dwelt alone. There were realms where only a mourning heart, a stranger or a quiet seeker for truth could find him. Herein, perhaps, was the secret of his power in opening the thought and life of that pathetic and brilliant girl, blind, deaf, and almost shut off from human understanding, Helen Keller. After his first talk by the pressure of her fingers in the hand of her interpreter, she said that she had always known there was a God, but had not before known his name. "The reason we love our friends is because God loves us," he wrote her: and they corresponded to the end of his life. Like many large people, he was sensitive to touch. "I won't call a doctor if I can help it," he once said to me, "for he will feel my pulse and I hate to be pawed over." And yet I have seen Helen Keller rush up to him, embrace him, and then with her sensitive hands and fingers touch every feature of his face and his head, and press his hands in signals, while he seemed to have forgotten his sensation in his interest in her pathetic yet happy soul.

Perhaps his most charming trait was his love of children. There was no suggestion of fear on their part; he was one of them, as cheery, simple and unconscious. I have seen him dart away from a company of clergymen and others on the piazza, march out upon the lawn, and with a child's trumpet lead the regiment around and around, with no thought of anything but the game. He caused consternation in the parsons' homes upon his visits or Episcopal visitations, rushing up stairs, snatching the babies out of their cribs, and bringing the children down to the parlor. The rector felt the precious hour towards which he had looked for a good talk vanishing in shouts and play. "Do you go to school?" he said to one of my children. "Yes." "Do you like it?" "No." "Then never go again. Tell your father and mother that the Bishop has told you that you need never go to school again. Never do anything that you don't want to." During supper at one of my early visitations a small child spoke up. "Why don't you talk to us? Bishop Brooks always talked to us."

The thrill and expectancy of teachers and children of the Sunday school as he came in to talk and close the service, would convince the coldest cynic that a child's nature was within him.

Far more charming than these incidents are his letters to his nieces and the children of the Sunday school.

Page after page runs on like these:

From Paris—
My dear Gertie,
   The funny thing is that the people here speak French. The little children about the streets speak it, just as well as you speak English. The boys and girls are very queer. The common little boys wear blue blouses, and the little girls wear small white night-caps all the time. It is bright sunshiny, and delightful.

From Berlin—
   The children in Paris all wore blouses, and the children in Venice did not wear much of anything. Here they all wear satchels. I never saw such children for going to school. The streets are full of them, going or coming all the time. They are queer little white-headed blue-eyed things, many of them very pretty indeed, but they grow up into dreadful-looking men and women. They wear their satchels strapped on their backs like soldiers' knapsacks,

and when you see a schoolful of three hundred letting out, it is very funny.

From Vienna—
Dear Gertie,

This letter is an awful secret between you and me. If you tell anybody about it, I will not speak to you all this winter. And this is what it is about. You know Christmas is coming, and I am afraid that I shall not get home by that time, and so I want you to go and get the Christmas presents for the children. The grown people will not get any from me this year. But I do not want the children to go without, so you must find out, in the most secret way, just what Agnes and Toodie would most like to have, and get it and put it in their stockings on Christmas Eve. Then you must ask yourself what you want, but without letting yourself know about it, and get it too, and put it in your own stocking, and be very much surprised when you find it there. And then you must sit down and think about Josephine De Wolf and the other baby at Springfield whose name I do not know, and consider what they would like, and have it sent to them in time to reach them on Christmas Eve. Will you do all this for me? You can spend five dollars for each child, and if you show your father this letter, he will give you the money out of some of mine which he has got. That rather breaks the secret, but you will want to consult your father and mother about what to get.

Life of Phillips Brooks

From India—

All the little girls, when they get to be about your age, hang jewels in their noses, and the women all have their noses looking beautiful in this way. I have got a nose jewel for you, which I shall put in when I get home, and also a little button for the side of Susie's nose, such as the smaller children wear. Think how the girls at school will admire you.

From Denver—

Dear Tood,

When I got here last night, I found the hotel man very much excited and running about waving a beautiful letter in the air, and crying aloud, "A letter from Tood! A letter from Tood!" He was just going to get out a band of music to march around the town and look for the man to whom the letter belonged, when I stepped up and told him I thought it was meant for me. He made me show him my name in my hat before he would give it to me, and then a great crowd gathered round and listened while I read it. It was such a beautiful letter that they all gave three cheers, and I thought I must write you an answer at once.

To Brooks's father and mother his life in Boston was of joy and comfort. The child love for his home and for them never faded. His mother had in the earlier years of his ministry feared for his faith, and she had prayed mightily that he might remain true. She warned him against a certain volume of sermons, "They tear the view of Christ's vicarious suffering all to pieces. I hope you do not own the book, but if you do, I want you to burn it with Frederick present to witness and exult over it." "No, my dear child; remember, you have promised to preach Christ and Him crucified in the true meaning of the words, and I charge you to stand firm." "Philly, I wish you would let Frederick read what I have written. It may do him good too. And excuse the plainness of my writing and impute it all to my love of the Truth and my earnest desire that you may continue Christ's faithful soldier and servant unto your life's end. Your faithful and affectionate friend and Mother."

Again and again in the back parlor in Hancock Street, she opened her heart to him, and she softened somewhat in her theology, while her pride in her boy increased with years. Strict in her theology, she was also a woman of sweet dignity and warmth of affection. William and Phillips dropped in often, but the house was empty; so the father and mother moved to the Phillips Homestead in North Andover, where Aunt Susan welcomed them. There the boys came for a night or for a longer stay in the summer. In 1879 the father fell asleep, and then a few months later the mother. To a friend Phillips wrote, "The happiest part of my life has been my mother, and with God's help she will be more to me than ever. The sense of God and His love has grown ever clearer in the midst of all this sadness and bereavement."

VIII

*Harvard University: Preacher, Overseer: system
of voluntary chapel prayers.—Honorary degree.*

IN LESS than three months after he had
taken charge of Trinity Church, Brooks began his spiritual work in Cambridge. On Brat-
tle Street, near Longfellow's house, stood the
new and beautiful St. John's Memorial Chapel
forming a part of the quadrangle of the Episcopal Theological School. On the evening of the
third Sunday in January, 1870, there was un-
wonted activity on the soft gravel sidewalks of
old Cambridge; Harvard students and profes-
sors, as well as residents who were unaccustomed to enter an Episcopal church, were moving toward St. John's. A junior at Harvard, I
was chairman of a committee to prepare for
them. We bought one hundred camp chairs for
the aisles: such a crowd had never been in the
chapel, or for that matter, had seldom gathered
in any Cambridge church. There was great curi-
osity to hear the young preacher whose prayer at
Commemoration was now a tradition. The ex-
periment of one evening service a month in

the chapel was so successful that it became an institution; and for seven years he preached to
a crowded congregation, delivering usually his
sermon of the morning. He also held a Bible
class of from twenty to forty students in the
basement of University Hall on certain week-
day evenings.

At the next Commencement, he was elected
an overseer of the university. Three years later
he preached his first sermon in Appleton Chapel.

Harvard was then under the traditional system of college religion. Attendance at daily
prayers by the students was compulsory; they
were also obliged to attend Sunday morning
service in some church or in Appleton Chapel
on Sunday evening. The Rev. Dr. Andrew P.
Peabody was the venerable pastor who had
charge of all chapel services and was Plummer
Professor of Christian Morals. He served the
college many years, and once told me that he
had taught in every subject of the curriculum
besides serving twice as acting President. Even
while he was alive and teaching, he had become
to the college world almost a tradition. After
his death, Brooks as an occasional preacher held
such sway as a spiritual leader that when a

vacancy occurred later, the college elected him to be pastor and professor. It was a momentous event in the academic life of New England, whose colleges had been administered upon a denominational basis. Harvard had been Unitarian by tradition and in the popular understanding, by law. President Eliot was a pronounced Unitarian as were a majority of the members of the Governoring Boards. The Episcopal Church from whose mother in England John Harvard had fled, had not been favored by the college. In spite of much questioning and criticism, these men with a deep sense of responsibility for the religious welfare of the students, put in the background their denominational preferences and elected a man whom they regarded as the greatest and most helpful spiritual leader.

As for Brooks, he had before him the most difficult question in his ministry to decide. In the consideration he took pains to make it clear that he was a Trinitarian and would remain loyal to his church's ministry. This was, of course, understood. His first intention was to accept. He had stood the wear and tear of parish life for twenty years, he had always looked with some envy upon the work of a scholar, and more than all, he wanted to concentrate his teaching, preaching, and leadership upon the youth and intellectual leaders of the country.

The question of his decision broadened in public interest. The college and President Eliot brought all reasonable pressure to bear; a mass meeting of students was held and letters pouring in from academic leaders over the country urged him to accept. On the other hand, his parish and representatives of the city and commonwealth presented the other side; a mass meeting of Boston young men was held; letters filled the columns of the newspapers. Brooks in much distress and doubt waited patiently for the waves of sentiment and arguments to pass; and several weeks later, after full and quiet deliberation, gave his decison to remain with his parish. The incident with its sharp differences of opinion and religious emotions latent with heat was closed with credit to all.

This and the changing conditions of college and religious life led to a fuller consideration of the whole subject of religion at Harvard. The elective system had placed all the studies upon a

voluntary basis; academic life and its exercises
had become ideally a privilege open to choice.
Why should religious observances remain compulsory and therefore irksome?

The students were becoming restless; evasions
at prayers and Sunday worship were becoming
habitual; petitions for the abolition of compulsory prayers were presented. At first Brooks,
who was by nature conservative and was a member of a committee of three overseers to study
and report, voted to stand by the old system.
Then after he had gone more deeply into the
subject, and had talked it over with officers
and students, he expressed his opinion at a
meeting of the overseers in favor of a voluntary system, and gave his reasons. That turned
the minority to a majority, and Harvard broke
from the New England collegiate tradition.
The action caused criticism and even dismay
in many quarters, and might have been rightly
condemned had not immediate action followed
looking towards a positive and vigorous system
in support of spiritual voluntary leadership. A
plan was carried through which has been in
operation ever since, whereby six ministers of
various denominations have, with one profes-

sor as chairman, been successively in residence throughout the academic year preaching on Sundays, and passing their mornings in the preacher's room ready to advise students who turn to them.

Brooks was a member of the first Board in 1886. He threw himself into the work with enthusiasm; preached to the students and officers thronging Appleton Chapel, and gave advice and inspiration to the students who for three hours each day of his residence came to him for consultation. The Board of Preachers planned to have only a short service every morning, but after the first week of Brooks's residence, the students insisted on a short address, and this became the custom. Special occasions, such as the opening of the college term, the Baccalaureate, the two hundred and fiftieth anniversary of Harvard, called him out with unusual power. At one time addresses were given to the students by leaders of several professions: Mr. Justice Holmes, for instance, on the Law. On the morning of the day when Brooks was to speak upon the Ministry, I met him looking worried. "What shall I say to those boys tonight?" He evidently had them on his soul. That evening

[133]

Sever II was packed to suffocation; students filled the chairs and aisles and stood crowded on the window sills; and Brooks, starting with an effort to be as cool and academic as Judge Holmes had been, was carried along with burning eloquence: He broke out, "I can't come here and talk to you of the ministry as one of the professions. I must tell you that it is the noblest and most glorious calling to which a man can give himself."

He was human: there were times when reactions came and he felt that he was accomplishing little; the disloyalty to ideals on the part of some one he had been trying to lead sent him into the depths of depression. And then he shook himself like a lion and took up the battle of life again. He served five years as preacher and twelve years as overseer.

It is an almost unbroken tradition that Harvard does not give an Honorary Degree to a member of its governing Boards, nor to anyone who is not present at Commencement to receive it. Under these conditions, the President and others felt that Brooks might go through life without giving an opportunity to the university to confer a degree upon him. Hence when he was abroad, and still an overseer, the President upon Commencement Day, 1877, conferred on him the degree of S.T.D. "in recognition of his eloquence as a preacher, his dignity and purity of life as a minister of religion, and his liberality and large-mindedness as a man."

IX

IN THE earlier years of his rectorship of Trinity Church, Brooks was in the habit of staying at his post through every other summer, and going to Europe the alternate summer. In this way he was able to reach a large number of Boston people and travelers who were passing through the city to and from the New England resorts, and at the same time prolong with a good conscience his vacations. He was an active traveler and sightseer, and in this way with six visits in twelve years, he covered practically the whole continent of Europe. By that time, he was beginning to feel the exhaustion, physical and mental and spiritual, coming from the persistent strain of preaching, work and excitement. His sermons, because of his rapid utterance, were in fact long, and made a heavier draft on his time and strength than those of most men: they were emotional as well as thoughtful: they, with the special addresses and speeches, kept his mind continually alert; whenever he was in company, much by way of talk was expected of him, and his entrance into any house was an occasion for excitement, especially if children were about. Hence the parish released him for a year's rest, and the gathering of fresh resources. After some time in Europe, he went to India, where he studied more deeply than the usual traveler, into the customs, religions, and missions; he preached from Henry Martyn's pulpit, and gained a fresh enthusiasm for Foreign Missions such as would have gladdened his mother. Although thousands of volumes of travel have been published since, his Letters of Travel stand up well in description, informality, and charm; those to his nieces are unique.

Later he went to Japan with his friend William McVickar, but it was almost impossible to get away from the solicitations and hospitalities of Americans and English in any country. One day he and McVickar determined to find a theater in Tokio, peculiarly Japanese. The giants sat down on the rug, folding their legs so far as they could, and with a sense of relief congratulated themselves that they were unknown, when an attractive young Japanese woman turned round and greeted Brooks as the honorary member of her class at Wellesley College. It was hopeless.

Each year closed and the next opened with a great Watch Night service, an innovation in those days, with the church crowded beyond the doors.

His sermons were no longer written, but preached after careful work without notes. This, of course, entailed greater mental and emotional strain: speeches followed frequently. I recall one great address in New York in 1883, upon the four hundredth anniversary of the birth of Martin Luther. From his Alexandria days he had held Luther in great honor as a reformer, a mystic, a leader in spiritual thought and life, who broke the shackles of medievalism, and brought the world into freedom of thought and liberty. New York's finest packed the old Academy of Music. I went with Henry Potter who had just been made Bishop. Brooks read from his manuscript until he came to the scene of the burning of the Pope's Bull, when he left his desk, came to the front of the platform, and launched a torrent of eloquence such as I have never heard even from him, and then returned to his manuscript. From time to time he published volumes of sermons which had a very large circulation; his one volume of theology was *The Influence of Jesus.*

While the output of sermon after sermon in Trinity and elsewhere never suggested the weight of routine, Brooks felt it from time to time. He welcomed change of subject and fresh faces. During a week in Lent, Wall Street, and indeed New York, was moved by noonday addresses of singular power and directness in Trinity Church, with a crowd pressing in from Broadway. Faneuil Hall in Boston was another center towards which the men of downtown moved; here again he gave of his best. St. Paul's Church on Tremont Street was crowded with men on Mondays at noon. He was so identified in the mind of the Church with preaching, that on the death of Bishop Paddock, his name as a successor, when first suggested, did not catch the influential men of the diocese. Those close to him, however, knew that he had administrative abilities, and of far greater importance, he had a personality, character, spiritual leadership, and a love of the commonwealth that would make of him a great Bishop of Massachusetts, and bring to the whole Church the worth of his prestige. Soon the people of the state realized that in him and his future they had a part. Letters filled the press commending him, and then the conservative representatives of the diocese began to take notice. In response to the objection that Brooks would not accept an election, his friends urged that only by his election could that be discovered; and they also knew that he was ready to consider this fresh channel of service to the state and to the whole Church. Three or four years before, he had been weakened by what was called a slow fever, and though his pace was now restored he would do a greater work in another field.

At the Convention of the Diocese in May, 1891, he was elected Bishop on the first ballot.

Then followed for two months an ordeal which might have undone a man of less faith and charity. Immediately upon his election came reports from here and there of his heretical opinions, his Unitarianism, his disloyalty to the Church. In spite of these charges, a majority of the standing committees throughout the Church gave consent without delay; there followed anonymous and signed protests against his confirmation, exaggerated statements, unfounded charges, and of course legitimate objections on the part of some by whose interpretation of the creeds and other standards of the Church Brooks was a heretic. Urged by some of his friends to define himself, he kept silent. To his friend Bishop Clark he wrote, "I will never say a word, or allow you to say a word, in vindication or explanation of my position. I stand upon my record, and by that record I will stand or fall. I have said what I think and believe in my public utterances and in my printed discourses, and have nothing to retract or qualify."

Finally, in July, a majority of Bishops consented and the day of consecration was appointed for October 14. Everything had conspired to make this service a great event. For the devotion to him of the mass of people had been kindled to heat by what they felt was an unwarranted persecution; and in this devotion multitudes of churchmen and his own friends joined. Hence wherever he went or spoke, crowds gathered. On October 4, the first Sunday of the term at Harvard, the chapel was packed to hear him preach from the text, "I am come that they might have life, and that they might have it more abundantly." A text that those who knew him can never hear without seeing a vision of his face, and hearing the sound of his voice. From Alexandria through Philadelphia, Boston, England, and Harvard, the abundant life in Christ had been his constant message.

On October 14, the crowd took possession of Copley Square. The commonwealth, the city, the Church, Bishops, clergy, and laity joined in the Consecration Service in Trinity Church. Standing opposite him in the chancel, I seemed to see his whole person and face transfigured with vital spiritual consecration as in answer to the challenge of the presiding Bishop, he said, "I am ready the Lord being my helper, I will so do by the help of God." At the close of the service the presiding Bishop, the senior in office, took the younger Bishop by the arm, and at the head of all, escorted him down the aisle to the west door.

From this moment a fresh spirit of consecration seemed to grip Phillips Brooks. Whether he felt that his time was short or not, he gave himself with complete abandonment to the work; thrice on Sunday and on week-days he visited churches throughout the diocese, which then included the whole state, preaching, confirming, ordaining, administering and advising. Standing beside him as some one asked for an evening address, I saw him turn over the leaves of his little engagement book and say, "I have not an evening for five months." Meanwhile his old parish, without a rector, called upon him for special duties and occasional services. By the laying on of his hands in Confirmation he came into a grateful, personal human touch unknown to a preacher. He made more visitations in eight months than had ever been made in a year in the American Church, indeed since St. Peter. When the General Convention met at Baltimore, he made a great address at Johns Hopkins University, turning the students' thoughts as ever towards the revelations of God soon to come, and closed, "Whatever happens, always remember the mysterious richness of human nature and the nearness of God to each one of us."

The outflow of physical strength, emotion, sympathy, friendliness and spiritual power was enormous, and exhausting. Dr. Weir Mitchell, coming from Philadelphia to visit his old friend (as he told me himself), said, "Phillips, you cannot go on like this. You have your choice, stop, be moderate, husband your strength and live a few years, or go on as you are, and die soon." Brooks sat silent for a few minutes, meditated, and then said, "Weir, I cannot stop now. I must go on." Better, he felt, a shorter life now, with intense consecration and service.

A visit to England the following summer gave change but no rest. He preached in the Abbey, and in cathedrals and churches, and was driven hither and yon; for the English who had read his sermons must meet the man. Upon his return, the pace became quicker; he went to General Convention, and chafing at the speeches and delays, turned to his friend Bishop Potter and said, "Henry, is it always as dull as this?"

Monday evening, January 2, 1893, he was at the Clericus for the last time, having come back that day from a visitation at Nantucket. During the reading of the essay, I watched him. He seemed to have grown old suddenly; he had been losing flesh; the furrows were deeper in his face and forehead; he was tired.

Three weeks later, on Monday morning, January 23, I went into town from Cambridge, and in Washington Street caught sight of a crowd standing and staring at a bulletin.

"Phillips Brooks is dead." I hurried to his house; it was of no use, crape was on the door-bell. I wandered about the streets; the city seemed to be standing still. Stranger said to stranger, friend to friend, "Phillips Brooks is dead." For three days there was deep depression at the sense of loss. Gradually the feeling became dominant that his work was done, that his life, though cut off at fifty-seven, was rounded out.

Though he was Bishop for only fifteen months, his was a great Episcopate. Under the faithful administration of Bishop Paddock, an organization had been built up which needed a great spiritual leader; it was waiting to be fused with life. The personality and preaching of Phillips Brooks did that. Many preachers and leaders are so personal and self-sufficient that when they are gone the cause droops. Brooks was so large, unselfish and unconscious of himself that when he had gone, the people, instead of dwelling on their loss, were grateful that he had been among them and took up the work where he left off. I know, for wherever I went a few months later, everyone accepted the situation, and "carried on" in the name of the Master to whom Brooks had led them.

In the next three days, there swept back to Boston from all parts of this country, from England, and from over the world, a wave of sorrow and gratitude which found expression later in great meetings of citizens in the cities, in subscriptions to memorials, and in Phillips Brooks House at Harvard.

January 25 was a day of sorrow and of exaltation. At twelve o'clock shops were closed, and the city swept down again to Copley Square. The body borne by eight Harvard students moved up the aisle. The service over, the procession passed out the west door, and the body rested upon a raised platform, while the great congregation filling the Square sang, "O God our help in ages past." Over the bridge to Cambridge the company went, and as they approached the College Yard, the bell which had called the students to chapel now called them out for the last service they could render him. They lined the Avenue on both sides as the procession passed between; at Mount Auburn the body was laid beside the grave of his mother, upon whose headstone Phillips had caused to be cut the words, "O Woman, great is thy faith. Be it unto thee even as thou wilt."

Index

Index

Index

[149]

Index

Index